TWELVE WHO FOLLOWED JESUS

Twelve Who Followed Jesus

landrum p. leavell

BROADMAN PRESS
NASHVILLE, TENNESSEE

4213-52
ISBN: 0-8054-1352-9

Dewey Decimal Classification: 225.92
Library of Congress Catalog Card Number: 74-18655
Printed in the United States of America

To the staff and membership of
First Baptist Church
Wichita Falls, Texas

CONTENTS

PREFACE

One great American suggested he was part of every man he had ever met. This is one way of stating the influence of others in life. The older one grows, the more he has to look back upon. For me, this backward look is inseparably connected with gratitude for a host of people who have contributed to my life and ministry.

My highest gratitude is due Jesus Christ, who loved me while I was yet a sinner and saved me when I was eight years old. The fact that he trusted me enough to call me to preach and give me challenging places of service is a humbling factor each day of my life.

This book on the twelve apostles was originally a series of sermons preached from the pulpit of the First Baptist Church, Wichita Falls, Texas. In the preparation of these messages I drew water from many wells. It is not possible to name everyone to whom I am indebted for insights and information. May my debt be acknowledged, though not repaid, by this simple statement. The study of the twelve was made in connection with a Sunday School attendance campaign in our church. Each Sunday for the twelve weeks one of the men of the church was dressed in a costume reminiscent of the first century, complete with beard and sandals! Each of these gave a personal testimony such as might have come from the lips of the actual apostle. Appearances were made in Sunday School classes, departments, and in the worship service, televised to thousands of people in the area.

Many younger persons were indelibly impressed by this visual presentation.

May these biographical sketches bless the hearts of all who read them. It is my prayer that the commitment of these men, in spite of human weaknesses like our own, will continually challenge and inspire Christians until our Lord returns.

Landrum P. Leavell

I
THE BIG FISHERMAN
Mark 1:17-18

Simon Peter was a typical young commercial fisherman. He was deft in the use of his hands, those same hands which were sometimes used in violence. His temperament had taken on the characteristics of the Lake of Gennesaret, or the Sea of Galilee, or the Sea of Tiberias as it is variously called in the New Testament. He was subject to ever-changing moods, and on occasion his temperament was fiery. He had a sharp tongue and all who knew him knew he had an opinion on every subject. He was not always right, but he was always vocal.

He was a colorful personality, and by today's standards he would be called an extrovert. He possessed many friends and natural leadership qualities that made him an outstanding personality.

Some have suggested that Simon Peter was a typical kid brother. He stands in marked contrast with Andrew, who was sober, mature, and steady, and whose personality could be counted on to be stable.

When Peter makes his first New Testament appearance, he is called Simon. This is the Gentile or Greek version of the name Simeon. On at least two occasions in the New Testament he is referred to as Simeon, which is the original Hebrew form of the name.

On occasion in the New Testament Peter is referred to as Cephas, for Jesus gave Simon a new name. The name Jesus gave him is ordinarily rendered Peter, from the Greek word *petros*. It means "rock." Cephas is the Aramaic version of that same word.

Keep in mind that most of the people in Jesus' day were at least bilingual, and many were trilingual. In our study of the New Testament we find Hebraisms, that is, words that have come into the Greek from Hebrew. The New Testament was written in Greek, but we also find strong traces of the Aramaic, the usual spoken language of first-century Palestine. Trilingual people understood things which to us are strange.

Simon was called Peter. Peter is a Greek name, Simon is from Hebrew. He is also called Cephas, the same as the word *petros* in Greek, which is the Aramaic word for rock. All these names might tend to be a little confusing to us, but they had no such effect on people in that day who were accustomed to two or more languages.

Down in the Rio Grande Valley of Texas most of the longtime residents have a good working knowledge of two languages. They speak Spanish and English fluently. This is because the land in which they live is so near to another nation. It's true on both sides of the border—in Mexico many speak English, and in Texas many speak Spanish. The same was true in the day of Jesus and Simon Peter. It was not unusual for an apostle to have two names. We'll see this in our study of the twelve.

We remember Thomas, who also was called Didymus. The name Didymus means twin, and that name, of course, causes questions to come rapidly to our minds. I wonder who Thomas' twin was? I wonder if Thomas was as faithful in witnessing to his twin brother as Andrew was in witnessing to his kid brother. I wonder if Thomas' twin might have died in childbirth or at an early age. He may not even have been alive when Jesus lived. I wonder what he missed?

There are other apostles who have dual names. Matthew was also called Levi. Nathanael Bartholomew is another one of the twelve, called Nathanael by some friends, Bartholomew by others.

A good friend of mine, R. H. Dilday, can tell by the name people call him where those friends knew him. If they knew him in Wichita Falls they call him H'ey, if they knew him at Baylor they call him R. H., and if they knew him in his ministerial life after seminary they call him Russell. This is not unusual, is it? In the book of Acts one woman goes by two names. She is called Tabitha and she is also called Dorcas. So we are talking about something most familiar in that day when we refer to this man Simon as Peter, or Cephas, or as Simon Peter.

All of this may well be a contrast, for Jesus gave him that name Peter or "Rocky." He said, "Thou art Simon Bar-jona." The word "bar" is a prefix which means "son of." Thou art Simon, son of Jona. An interesting sidelight is the name Jona, which means "dove." Now most of us have some familiarity with that bird, and we happen to know a dove is a fluttering, dipping, ever-changing bird. Some of you had the same experience recently I had. That is, you looked up on the horizon and saw a dove coming straight toward you from a long way off. Your heart began to beat a little faster and your gun was in the ready position. You didn't move until the last moment, but then the dove changed course. You missed the shot, for you didn't have an opportunity. That's characteristic of a dove, and they knew about doves in Jesus' day. When Jesus said to Peter, "Thou art Simon, son of Dove," He may have been alluding to the fluctuating nature of Peter's character. He stated he would name him "Rocky," Peter the Rock. That might have drawn a laugh from those who knew Simon. Perhaps like calling a baldheaded man "Curly," or a fat man "Slim," or a tall man "Shorty." It had the same effect when Jesus said, "Thou art Simon Bar-jona, and I'm going to name you Rock."

Now Simon lived up to his nickname rather than having to live it down. In the end, as we find him described in the pages of the New Testament, he was precisely what Jesus said he would be. He was as solid and stable as a rock.

Let's go back to the text and remember the—

Invitation

—extended Simon. Peter was a fisherman and it was from his boat and nets that Jesus called him. We find in this invitation something of the purpose of our Lord, for he wasn't merely calling men to be his followers. In this and other notable instances Jesus was calling men who would first be trained and then would disciple others. I believe that's the call Jesus extends to us, for he wants us not merely to be saved; he wants us to be involved in the redemptive process of telling the world about salvation. He's never called anyone to live in isolation or seclusion from the rest of the world, for he so pointedly said, "Ye shall be witnesses unto me." Whoever we are, under whatever circumstances we may have been saved, it is our high commitment and responsibility to be faithful in sharing the Word.

As we read the New Testament, if we read it in isolation, it may seem that Jesus one day walked by the table where Matthew was collecting taxes and simply extended a hand to him and commanded him to come and follow him. It may seem to the casual reader that this was the first encounter Matthew ever had with Jesus, but when we read the New Testament in context and get the total picture, we find the likelihood that it was not Matthew's first contact with our Lord. It seems that Simon, Matthew, and all the twelve went through stages in becoming apostles.

In the first stage these people were disciples, and a disciple is a learner. Jesus Christ had myriads of disciples. He had only twelve apostles. The apostles, according to the meaning of the Greek word, a combination of *apo* and *stello*, were those "sent away from." That is, they came to Jesus, they learned from him and then were sent out to do a specific task. Disciples were learners. In that sense you and I are disciples. We've not been called to this unique ministry to which Jesus called twelve men, we're not called to be apostles, but we are called as disciples or learners. In the first stage Peter, Andrew, James, John, Matthew, and the rest of the twelve were learners. They were disciples and followed Jesus only on occasions.

Some of those occasions that come to mind include the wedding at Cana of Galilee. It was there that the friends of Jesus gathered with him for the festive occasion, and they could scarcely slake their thirst. They were so thirsty in that hot, dry land, they soon consumed all of the refreshments. Mary, the mother of Jesus, turned to our Lord and told him they had a problem. Jesus in turn alleviated the problem by performing the miracle of changing water into wine. Peter, Andrew, James, John, and some of the others were with our Lord on that occasion. At another time they observed the Passover in Jerusalem prior to being called apostles. Some of these apostles were there as disciples only.

At a second stage of development, fellowship with Christ became uninterrupted. These men forsook their jobs in secular employment and stayed with our Lord continuously day and night. Undoubtedly, large numbers of people did just that. Everywhere Jesus went multitudes of people followed him. When on occasion they were separated from him, the New Testament reveals they tried to find where he was and get there as quickly as they could. There may have been thousands who had forsaken their jobs, who found in Jesus the fulfillment of the messianic promises, and who felt that the kingdom was coming and the consummation of the age had been reached.

Then there was the third stage of development. That was when Jesus Christ handpicked twelve men. He called them to a specific task, singled them out to become a select band, and trained them for the work of apostleship.

It's likely that Peter, Andrew, James, and John, these fishermen, had been followers of John the Baptist. They certainly were not ignorant of the messianic promises. In fact, when Andrew shared his faith he said, "We have found the Messias, which is being interpreted, the Christ" (John 1:41). Jesus was the fulfillment of prophecy, and they proclaimed that fact as they shared their faith with other people.

When Jesus became identified as the Messiah they began to follow him. It was on the basis of their growing conviction that Jesus was the One that Peter and the others answered the call to apostleship.

Our text gives us the fullest account of the call of Simon Peter. In Luke 5:1-2 we read that our Lord, pressed by the throng, crowded down to the water's edge at the Sea of Galilee, called for Simon

Peter to lend him his boat. He stepped into the prow of the boat, was pushed out from the land, and there he addressed a vast audience. If he had remained on the shore, crowded close to the water, and had tried to teach from that position, only those closest to him could have heard. You know, it's of more than passing interest to recall that water has a real loudspeaker effect. Your voice can be heard farther over water than it can over land, and Jesus pushed out in the boat and used that natural loudspeaking system formed by the waters of the Sea of Galilee to teach a multitude of people.

After he had finished the sermon Jesus turned to Simon and said, "Launch out into the deep and let down your nets for a draught." Simon began to argue. He protested that there wasn't any need. The signs weren't right, the moon was not full, they had had rains recently, the barometric pressure was not conducive to good fishing, and the fishing meter on the boat says that there aren't. . . . Well, whatever he said, the fishing wasn't good!

Maybe Peter didn't have the methods that some of you have in determining when the fish ought to bite or where the fish are, but he said it was useless. "Master, we have toiled all the night, and have taken nothing." Then he turned to our Lord and said, "Nevertheless, at thy word I will let down the net." He put out from the land, let down his net again, and caught so many fish the net broke. In response to that phenomenal catch they had to call for the other boat and the other two brothers to come out and help them bring the catch to land. When they reached the shore Simon fell at the feet of Jesus, clasped his knees, and cried out, "Depart from me; for I am a sinful man, O Lord." He recognized in humility the supernatural knowledge of Jesus Christ and his own sinfulness.

Jesus said, "Fear not, from henceforth thou shalt catch men." That was his invitation. Think with me for a moment about his—

Imperfections.

The Sea of Galilee is subject today to sudden, violent storms. The Golan Heights are just a little to the north, and over those mountains flow air currents that descend upon the Sea of Galilee and often become violent and tempestuous. On one occasion the apostles were in a boat on the Sea of Galilee when a storm struck. They could not reach the land. You recall their fear. They cried out in fear, and these men were seasoned seamen. Suddenly they looked up and saw Jesus walking to them on the water. Simon immediately wanted to share in that experience and asked our Lord if he could come to him on the water. That his faith was faulty is proved as he began to sink into the waves and cried out for help.

In many of the New Testament accounts of Peter, we see him in contrast. He was both brave and cowardly, wise and foolish, fearful and fearless, open-minded and closed-minded, a man of doubt and a man of faith. He was impulsive and uninhibited, often speaking before he thought. Simon Peter is a real paradox, yet his very imperfections make him lovable because we can identify with this man.

He was a man of action, never satisfied with talk. He was not the kind of man who would have been content to sit in committee meetings. He wanted to get out and put the plans to work. He clasped the knees of Jesus in unfeigned humility, he walked on the water, he wanted to remain on the mount of transfiguration, start a construction program, and build three tabernacles.

When our Lord was taken by soldiers of the high priest, it was Simon Peter who drew a sword and cut off the ear of one soldier. I'll always believe he was trying to cut off his head, but in the darkness misjudged and the man's life was spared. Simon Peter was a man of action.

One day after the first Easter morning, he saw the risen Lord standing on the shore of the Sea of Galilee. He couldn't wait for the slow boat to get to shore, so he jumped in and swam to shore that he might greet and kiss the risen Christ. Thank God for a man like Peter, a man who thinks big and who wants to do a big thing for the Lord Jesus and his kingdom.

Now there are some other things about this man that we must understand. I want you to remember his—

Insights.

Peter had a spiritual perception which is enviable. He, out of the twelve, was the only one who understood fully the identity of Jesus Christ. He knew who Jesus was and was not afraid to state it. What a matchless moment that must have been to hear Jesus Christ say, "Blessed art thou, Simon Bar-jona: for flesh and blood hath not revealed it unto thee." It was a moment of spiritual insight and deep spiritual perception. Simon had identified Jesus as the Christ, the Son of the living God, and Jesus responded that this was the foundation upon which his kingdom would be established. That's the foundation upon which his church is built and all of the forces of hell will not be able to withstand the onrush and conquest of his church.

Some people misunderstand this passage and claim that the rock on which the church is established is the man Simon Peter. The fact is, everyone who enters the kingdom of God has to make the same confession Simon made. It's only when we know Jesus Christ as the Son of the living God, the fulfillment of all of the Old Testament prophecies, the one whom God promised, that we become Christians and enter the kingdom. So the church is not built upon Simon. The church is built upon Jesus the Christ.

Isn't it interesting to note the sequel in that text from Matthew? Immediately following that high point in the life of Peter, that moment of great spiritual insight, he sank to the depths. Jesus began to explain to his apostles that he would have to go to Jerusalem and there be called upon to suffer and die, and that men would abuse him. Do you remember what Peter said? In his hostility, his readiness for a fight, he began to draw himself taut and said, "Be it far from thee, Lord: this shall not be unto Thee" (Matt. 16:22). Jesus turned, realizing that Simon's insight of just a short time before was now gone, and said, "Get thee behind me, Satan."

Peter couldn't believe that the Christ of God would suffer the abuse of human beings and give his life in Jerusalem. What a change there was in the mood and attitude, but how typical this is of the Big Fisherman. Yet he leaves us a pattern of unswerving faith. What a wonderful pattern that is.

Our Lord gave Simon Peter a final exam. Most of us would be prone to conclude that the final would have to do with doctrine. After all, if Simon and others of the twelve were not well grounded in the things of the faith, what chance would the kingdom of God have? If these men were not doctrinal, if they didn't know the bedrock foundation of the things of the kingdom, how could the church succeed? How could the kingdom ever cover the earth as waters cover the sea? If we had been making out this examination for Jesus Christ to give Simon Peter, most of us would have made it doctrinal in its thrust. But that wasn't what Jesus did. As important as doctrine is, we must never forget the importance of emotions. Every one of the three questions that Jesus asked Peter had to do with his emotions: "Peter, do you love me?"

You see, you can hold all of the proper doctrines flawlessly and with perfect orthodoxy, and still be unloving and unkind and stingy in your heart. You can know all of the right things, you can be "a Baptist through and through," but that's not enough. The important thing is, do you love Jesus? Three times Jesus had to ask Simon Peter, "Lovest thou me?" Each time Simon responded affirmatively. When the third question was asked Simon was perplexed, but resorted to the court of highest appeal. He said, "Lord, thou knowest all things; thou knowest that I love thee." How many times I've read that verse! How many times I have wondered in my heart if I would really be content to leave my love in the hands of the knowledge of the Son of God.

If Jesus were to ask me, "Do you love me?" I'd have to admit that my faith is weaker than Peter's. There are times when I believe my life may reveal genuine, true love for Jesus, but there are also times when I, like Simon Peter, have betrayed my Lord and out of cowardice failed to take my stand for his glory.

All of us can identify with Peter, but let me remind you of one other thing. In Luke 22:61 we find the end of that story of the denial of Peter with this sentence, "And the Lord turned and looked upon Peter." With one look from the eyes of Jesus, Peter was restored to warmth and fellowship.

You can never convince me that his look was one of censure or condemnation. I know in my heart it was a look of tenderness, of mercy and forgiveness. You see, I too, have experienced that kind of look. When I was down in the very depths of despair, when cowardice ruled my life, when I had failed, as you sometimes fail, I found that the look of Jesus is a look of forgiveness. This is common in the Christian experience. And so with one glance Jesus seemed to say to Simon Peter that it was all right. He was forgiven. Now there were new and greater things for him in the future. He was not to look back but look up, look forward, and live from that moment. It's that experience in the life of this incomparable apostle that gives hope to you and me.

That's the reason that we can say with James Montgomery: "When thou seest me waver, with a look recall, nor for fear or favor suffer me to fall."

When we fall we can stand again and receive that look of forgiveness and pardon based on our repentance. When we, like Peter, weep those bitter tears knowing we have done our Lord a disservice, his look draws us back to him in warmth and fellowship.

II
ANDREW—WORTHY MISSIONARY
John 6:5-14

It's regrettable that we don't have more authoritative information about the twelve apostles, but we can be grateful for what we do have. The man whom we study now, Andrew, is mentioned fourteen times in the pages of the New Testament. Without debate, he is one of the most deserving men described in God's Word. Through the various incidents in which we find Andrew prominently mentioned we can gain insights into his character and be strengthened by his witness.

John's Gospel tells us Andrew was a fisherman who lived in the village of Bethsaida, close to the city of Capernaum. This was also the home of other notable fishermen who were called to be apostles, and this community has great significance in New Testament history. Like his brother Simon, Andrew was invited to follow Jesus Christ and to become a fisher of men.

Let's take the evidence we have regarding this apostle, piece it together, and see if we can get a composite picture. I'd like for us initially to recall his—

Selection.

Andrew, along with John, was among the first to attach himself to Jesus. Our Lord embarked on his earthly ministry following the time of his baptism in the Jordan River by John the Baptist. After that he began to call men to follow him. This was not the call to apostleship. It was a call to discipleship. The word "disciple" means

learner, so he invited men to follow him and become learners of
his way.

At a later time in his earthly ministry, Jesus called twelve men
to be apostles. These had unique, distinct places in our Lord's kingdom and in the outreach ministry after his resurrection.

Almost all the information we have about Andrew is found in
John's Gospel. This probably indicates a warm, personal relationship
between these two men. They were present when John was baptizing,
and they heard him identify Jesus when he came to the Jordan to
be baptized. You'll recall that word of introduction. John, in the
Jordan River, saw Jesus coming and said, "Behold the Lamb of God,
that taketh away the sin of the world." We've heard that quotation
so many times it just rolls off without much impression. That was
a startling, electrifying statement! You see, John the Baptist was
identifying Jesus as the One of whom the Old Testament prophets
had prophesied. When he referred to him as the Lamb of God, he
was tying together all of the strings of prophecy. He identified Jesus
as the One whom God had prepared from before the foundation
of the world.

In the Old Testament the sins of mankind were absolved or forgiven
on the basis of animal sacrifice. The blood of a lamb was offered
for the absolution of sins of an individual. That sacrifice, a lamb
without any flaw, without spot or blemish, was acceptable to God
when offered in the right spirit for the sins of that individual.

At a later time in Old Testament history, in the progression of
God's plan and revelation, the blood of an animal was offered for
the sins of a nation. You'll recall that the high priest, one time each
year on the Day of Atonement, entered into the holy of holies in
the Temple in Jerusalem bearing the blood of a lamb without spot
or blemish for the sins of the nation.

In God's eternal revelation, John the Baptist identified Jesus Christ
as the Lamb of God that takes away the sins of the world! Not
one man or one family, not one nation, but for the sins of all mankind
who come to God through Jesus Christ. That identification was so

implicit, so complete, that immediately Andrew and John understood what John the Baptist was saying. They turned from being followers of John the Baptist to follow Jesus Christ. They became disciples or learners.

It's not unusual in the literature of the first century to find Andrew referred to by the Greek word *protokletos*, which means "first called." He was among the first called to be a disciple. This does not imply that no one was saved before Jesus was baptized, but it means that in the earthly ministry of our Lord, Andrew was among the first called to follow the Lord Jesus Christ.

This apostle encourages the hearts of most Christians. When we study his life there is no indication he was a ten-talent man. I'm intimidated when I study the life of the apostle Paul. He intimidates me because of his many talents. Think of the things that Paul could do. He could preach in an incomparable fashion. He could expound the Scriptures as only the most learned of rabbis could do. He had the personal charisma to challenge the people to give even their lives for Jesus Christ.

There is no indication of this kind of talent in Andrew's life. We don't have any suggestion that he was a five-talent man. The only talent the New Testament reveals which he possessed was the talent of being friendly. He was just an outgoing man who made friends easily. Any time you find Andrew in the New Testament, he is in the company of one or more individuals. He's never found alone. He must have been a friendly person.

When we contrast Andrew with other apostles, we learn he never preached like his own blood brother Simon Peter. He never recorded a gospel as did Matthew and John. He never traveled widely over the known world like Paul, nor was he ever recognized by the church as was James. There's nothing about Andrew to compare with the lives of some of the others, but Jesus called Andrew and Simon Peter to be "fishers of men." Andrew became the dynamic personal soul-winner while his brother Simon Peter became the magnetic mass evangelist.

In our society, God has chosen only one man to serve in the capacity Billy Graham fills. There's not another Billy Graham. There's not another man upon whose shoulders the mantle of God's power has resided as it does upon him.

At the National Prayer Breakfast for foreign missions in Dallas on November 30 we heard the testimonies of a number of missionaries. The thrilling thing each of the missionaries from different parts of the world talked about was the evident revival taking place now. We're in a period of spiritual resurgence or renaissance unparalleled in history.

A missionary to Korea, one of our Southern Baptist missionaries, told of things taking place in that part of the world. He said the largest gathering of human beings for any event in the history of the world was seen not many months ago when more than one million persons gathered, not for a sporting event, not for some national holiday, but to hear the gospel of Jesus Christ. They came to hear Billy Graham tell the story of Jesus. We think it's something special when 105,000 football fans gather to see their favorite teams play football. Listen, big things are happening today in response to the movement of God's Spirit, and they'll continue to happen. Yet in all the world God has hosen only one man to be the evangelist filling the place Billy Graham fills.

Where God has chosen one evangelist he has chosen multiplied thousands like you and me to follow Andrew in personal soul-winning. We can be friendly, outgoing people with the ability to shake hands and make another person feel comfortable in our presence, and then we can share the faith and relate the good news of Jesus Christ. Jesus needed a man like Andrew in the apostolic fellowship, and his selection is more than justified by his contribution.

In churches everywhere Jesus Christ needs people like you, who may not be ten-talent persons, but who have the talent of friendliness, who are warmhearted, outgoing people who can speak to another person and make him feel at home. Thank God for Andrew. Thank God for the wisdom of eternity which caused his selection.

Think with me for a moment about the—

Service

—he rendered as recorded in the New Testament. In three of the appearances of Andrew in the New Testament he is applying the stock-in-trade of the Christian. He is found introducing someone else to Jesus Christ. Let's look at those three experiences.

In the first he brought his own kinsman, Simon Peter, to Jesus. Of course he was not named Peter until after he was saved, but Simon was the first one Andrew brought to our Lord. Thank God for Andrew, who understood that the business of the Christian faith begins at home! That's where it ought to begin with us. Why is it we're so hesitant about sharing the faith with members of our families?

I've had many wives come to me in concern over their lost husbands, requesting that I share the faith with that husband. Almost without exception they say, "You can't approach my husband the same way you would other men." I don't understand why, but every woman with a lost husband thinks her husband is different. I don't know any different approach to be made, for the Bible says all of us have sinned and come short of the glory of God. That lost husband will never be saved until he admits his sin and repents of it. There's no new approach to be made. Surely that husband is an individual. He has a personality different from the personality of every other person, but the Christian gospel has a common denominator. To that common denominator every saved person must come. It's an acknowledgment of sin. It's repentance from sin and turning to Jesus Christ in faith and trust. Simon Peter was the first man brought to Christ by a home missionary. The home missionary was his own brother Andrew. Thank God for a man like that.

Sometimes people come to me and request that I witness to a certain person. They say, "Preacher, this person is lost and needs to be saved. I want you to go and talk with that one about Jesus. But don't you dare tell him I sent you!" Why not? Are you ashamed of your faith? Are you afraid of your own inconsistent Christian life? Are you fearful that such a person would laugh and sneer that you, of all people, would be the one wanting him to be saved? Andrew apparently didn't have any such hangup. He wanted his own brother to know Jesus Christ and share the joy he found in him. Andrew was the first home missionary, and his example stands as a challenge to all of us.

Edward Kimball was a successful merchant in Boston. Once he found a young man selling shoes in a shoe store, and shared the faith with him. That young man was from the country, he was poor, without family, friends, or funds. Kimball took him to Sunday School and later he was converted. Not long after that, the young man moved from Boston to Chicago. Today all the world knows the witness and testimony of Dwight L. Moody, one of the greatest evangelists of any generation. He is the man who, in the power of God it is said, took one continent in one hand and another continent in the other hand and brought them together in Jesus Christ.

Andrew never was the preacher Simon Peter was, but he shared every victory Peter won because he brought Simon to Christ. It's likely that Andrew had personally won to Christ some of the people who made decisions when Peter preached at Pentecost. I'm sure Andrew was in that group of 120 who prayed before Pentecost and who went out under pentecostal impulse to share the faith with the entire city of Jerusalem. I'm certain some of those three thousand who made public decisions had been led to know Jesus through the witness of this man Andrew.

In the second incident we find Andrew bringing a lad to Jesus, a little boy who had five biscuits and a few fish. What discernment and faith it must have demanded to see an insignificant lad and a meager sack lunch holding great possibilities of service in the kingdom. A lot of us, as busy as we are, would have overlooked that restless lad with his sack lunch, but not Andrew. Or if we had not overlooked him, we would have been irritated by him and we would have asked, "What does that kid want to come out here for?

He can't even be still. He's not even listening. He's rattling his sack with the lunch in it. Why doesn't somebody do something about that kid?" Andrew saw in that youngster a tremendous potential for kingdom service. He had the ability to discern human potential. What a marvelous quality to possess.

Who knows but that in our Sunday School or yours there may be a Billy Graham or a Dwight L. Moody! You may be the one who has the discernment to put an arm of love around the shoulders of such a youngster and encourage him in the faith and let him know that older people are interested in him and love him and want him to be all that he can possibly be in Christ's service. Such concern could change the direction of a whole life.

In the third appearance of Andrew bringing others to Jesus, we find he became the first "foreign" missionary. He brought some Greek-speaking people to Jesus. Unlike his brother Simon, who would not preach in the home of a Gentile without taking certain witnesses with him, he brought these Greek-speaking men to Christ without hesitance. Would to God that we'd grasp the gospel in the same way Andrew did. He understood that the gospel wasn't just for Jews. He knew it was for anyone, regardless of the color of his skin, regardless of the language he spoke with his tongue, regardless of his culture or nationality. Andrew knew the gospel crossed over barriers of race, geography, and nationalism.

Thank God, Andrew knew Jesus so well he knew there was no human being whom Jesus would refuse to see, nor was there any moment of the day when Jesus was too busy to talk to a troubled person. Would to God we used that example. Most of the time when troubled people come around, we want to go in the other direction. We don't have time to listen to them. We don't have time to share the faith. We're too busy to deal with people like that, but Andrew wasn't, and the Christ Andrew served was never too busy either.

Andrew would have made an ideal head usher. He knew exactly what to do with visitors. He knew where to take them. The service of Andrew was an outgrowth of his spirit.

Think about that—

Spirit.

Although Andrew appears to be completely overshadowed by his brother, there is no suggestion of jealousy or bitterness. It takes a great deal of grace to play second fiddle, more especially when it's one's own brother by whom he is totally overshadowed. No one likes to be known as "so-and-so's brother." I imagine Andrew was frequently introduced as Simon's brother. That's irritating, isn't it?

This is roughly equivalent to a man being introduced as "Mrs. So-and-so's husband." You don't like that, do you? You swell up a little if someone introduces you in that way.

Recently I visited my folks in Newnan, Georgia. I went into a place of business where a lady looked up, smiled, and said, "Oh, yes, you're Margaret Mann's brother, aren't you?" Well, that was something new. I don't get that very often. I'm not known as Margaret Mann's brother in Wichita Falls. I have my own identity, so this struck me. It's interesting to go back home. You know, they don't know what's happened to me, where I've been, or who I am! I'm just Landrum Leavell in Newnan, and everybody, black and white said, "Hello, Landrum." Then too, when in the company of others and someone calls, "Hey, Preacher," I always turn around! I'm not the preacher over there. I'm just Landrum Leavell who grew up there. It's different.

It's easy to get jealous and become bitter over little matters like that, but Andrew didn't. Andrew knew Jesus first and introduced Simon Peter to him, but he had the rare humility which kept him from being resentful. That's the same spirit that characterizes members of this church who week after week serve Jesus Christ faithfully, who prepare diligently, who attend regularly, who serve humbly and without recognition. Their only concern is to render service for the Lord Jesus Christ.

There's a strong tradition which holds that Andrew, after preaching over a wide geographical area, even parts of Russia, finally was put to death at a ripe old age in Greece. This tradition maintains that his death came after he had led Maximilla, the wife of the Roman proconsul Aegeas, to know Christ. Aegeas became so enraged over the fact that his wife had become a Christian, he ordered Andrew to lead in offering sacrifices to a heathen god. When he refused, Andrew was beaten severely, tied to a cross, and crucified. That cross, shaped like an X, is today called Andrew's cross. As he lingered there for two whole days before death came, he preached the gospel of Jesus Christ to all who came by, exhorting them to repentance and faith.

There is a wonderful, magnetic appeal about this man Andrew, for though life placed him in a position to become bitter, resentful, and antagonistic, he was nevertheless content to accept second place and serve Jesus Christ faithfully from that point.

Following Andrew's example, you and I have the opportunity of getting to know Jesus and introducing him to someone else. In the divine economy this is big business, and we are involved.

III
JAMES—CHRISTIAN MARTYR
Acts 12:1-2

The name James is common in the New Testament. There are at least three different men who go by that designation. The first of these is James, the brother of John, the beloved apostle. This James is said to be a son of Zebedee. He, his brother John, Peter, and Andrew are the four most prominently mentioned apostles in the Gospels.

The second of these is also an apostle named James, the son of Alphaeus, often referred to as James the Less. By comparison with the James whom we are studying now, he was the lesser known of the two.

The third James mentioned in the New Testament is the half brother of our Lord, who came into great prominence and recognition in the early church following the resurrection of our Savior. You'll recall that the Gospels picture the half brothers and half sisters of Jesus as cool toward the ministry of our Savior and indifferent to his appeals.

On one occasion it was Jesus' own half brothers and half sisters (with the same mother but not the same father) who came with Mary, his earthly mother, thinking that he was deranged or demented, and tried to draw him apart from his teaching ministry.

Obviously there was a great change in attitude on the part of James, the half brother of our Lord, for the New Testament tells us he became a pillar in the church, a leader, a man among men.

The truth of the matter is none of the twelve received much

biographical notice in the New Testament. We don't have any lengthy description of their lives and ministries. We catch glimpses of them as they ministered with our Lord and following his resurrection. This does not, however, lessen our desire to know everything we can about them, and we have two main sources of information. One of these is the New Testament. The other is tradition.

On each of the twelve beautiful windows of our church there is the name of one apostle. Based on what we learn from both tradition and the New Testament, there are symbols representing the apostles on the windows. These symbols are well-known in Christian history. One can notice that each symbol is different.

It would seem, as we try to learn what we can of the apostles, that they were a band of poor, illiterate, Galilean peasants. They were utterly devoid—as people ordinarily conceive it—of any social consequence. They weren't known by the leaders in the land. They didn't have any prominence in the communities in which they lived. They were almost totally obscure individuals. Why, under heaven, would Jesus choose men like this? I think this really is one of the most encouraging aspects of the Christian gospel. On the same basis which Jesus chose them, he chose you and me, and we fall into that same category.

This is not the best type of reasoning for every situation, but I want to begin with a conclusion as we try to determine why Jesus chose them. My conclusion, which governs everything else I might think or learn about these twelve men, is that our Lord chose them in the perfect wisdom of God. Jesus was perfect. He was God himself, and so it was with that wisdom, that omniscience that he hand-picked twelve men. Don't think for a moment that he was taken by surprise with the rejection of Judas. Jesus knew that he was an unsaved, unregenerate individual.

Among the other lessons we may learn from Judas, perhaps our Lord was trying to say to us that even among those who profess the name of Christ and who belong to the church of the Lord Jesus there will be those who are not saved. Judas wasn't, yet it was in the wisdom of God that these twelve men were chosen.

Moving from that foundation, why would Jesus pick men like this? Surely it was not hometown pride that caused him to pick mostly Galileans. It wasn't nepotism, or partiality to kinfolks, that made him choose some who probably were his earthly, fleshly cousins. It was not a renunciation of education or wealth or culture that moved him to choose poor, uneducated men.

Why did Jesus choose these particular ones? The only conclusion I can draw is that these were the only ones available. Is not this the same procedure we follow in the kingdom today? By all means we would prefer to have persons who have a good theological background to teach in our Sunday School, but oftentimes those persons who have the highest degrees in their chosen professions or disciplines are unavailable. They simply won't accept these responsibilities. They won't fulfill functions within the organization, and we are forced to take what is available. God blesses this availability, and those who don't have quite as much formal education but who are willing to serve often are used in marvelous and magnificent ways in the work of the kingdom. Jesus chose what was available. These men were willing, and that's a prime requisite in kingdom service.

Others may have been too proud or too busy or too ashamed to follow our Lord and become apostles. Even today we find this is true in far too many cases, for persons with a rich educational background or with the wealth of this world simply aren't available. They don't have time, or they don't want to serve, or they're not willing to give themselves in capacities like this. Sometimes such persons have little sense of personal need and almost no sense of personal repentance.

On the other hand there are persons who fall into that category who are usable. The apostle Paul is one who comes to mind, for in the apostle Paul, God found a highly educated, highly articulate, wealthy individual who had a background of culture, and who had received the best education open to him in that day. When Christ needed a proponent of the gospel in the first century to give it its greatest springboard into the known world, he selected a man who had both wealth and education.

Let's think for a moment about the—

Personality

—of this man James. The only way we can determine this is by gleaning bits of information about his behavior. Jesus referred to James and his brother John as "sons of thunder." The fact that the name James appears first in the listings of these brothers may indicate that James was the older of the two. Just as in the case of Andrew compared to Simon Peter, James was the lesser known of the two. John, the brother of James, is the author of five New Testament works. He is the author of the Gospel of John, the three Johannine epistles, and the Revelation. From that standpoint he completely overshadowed his brother James, yet the mention of the name James first in sequence indicates that he may have been the older.

When you name your children do you start with the youngest and move up to the oldest? Around our place we always mention Lan first for he's the oldest, and usually in sequence David is the last: Lan, Ann, Roland, and David. That's the way God gave them to us, and that's the way we refer to them. You're accustomed to this, so in all probability when James' name is consistently mentioned first it probably indicates he was the older of the two.

Some scholars say the title "sons of thunder" did not refer to James and John, but to their father, Zebedee. I suppose Zebedee had a right to blow his top. He could well have been called "Old Thunderhead." You see, he was the owner of a very successful fishing business. These commercial fishermen had just had the greatest bonanza they had ever had. They had such a fantastic catch the nets couldn't contain the fish. The nets broke.

Simon Peter was working as hard as he could with Andrew, but James and John had to go out in their boat to help them bring in that tremendous draught of fish. Just after they landed that catch,

Jesus told James and John he would make them fishers of men. They turned and waved goodbye to Zebedee, and followed Jesus. What do you think he did? I imagine he started pulling his hair out! I expect he stomped his feet, if he was that kind of person. He may have cursed a little, because most of the fishermen I have known do that once in awhile. Are you one of those? Yes, some are suffering from smitten consciences. It could be this title referred to Zebedee rather than to the two sons, but while a possibility, in my judgment it's far more likely that the boys were the ones who deserved the title.

Remember some experiences from the life of Jesus and his apostles. One time they were on their way southward to Jerusalem, passing through Samaria. You are familiar with the Samaritans. They fought with the Jews like cats and dogs. If you were going south through Samaria on the way to Jerusalem to worship, you were *persona non grata* as a Jew going through Samaria. If you were going northward, leaving the Temple and worship, they looked upon you in a different way. You were acceptable to pass through their land. The hatred was such that Jews, after having walked through the country of Samaria, would get to the border and stomp their feet to shake the dust of Samaria off their sandals. They didn't even want Samaritan dust clinging to their feet. That was the attitude which prevailed.

Jesus and his twelve disciples were going southward toward Jerusalem. They were tired; the close of day had come, and they needed some overnight accommodations. Jesus sent several of the disciples into Sychar, near the present-day city of Nablus, to inquire about the possibility of getting a place to spend the night. I don't know what happened. It may have been that the residents were inhospitable. They may have made the disciples mad. On the other hand, the disciples might have been overbearing. They might have gone in, telling the folks what they were going to do and how they were going to do it, and demanding what they had to have, and right now! The outcome of the matter was they were refused accommodations. When the disciples came outside the town to meet Jesus, they described what had taken place. James, son of thunder, said, "Lord, rain down fire on this town." He wanted them wiped off the face of the earth. Who did they think they were, treating the apostles like this? Son of thunder, James had a violent temper. Like so many of us, James got mad at the wrong things. He got mad at people instead of causes. That's an easy trap to fall into, isn't it?

How many persons can you name whom you really resent? I mean people at whom you are mad. If you can name a single one, I can guarantee you're out of fellowship with Jesus. If there is one single person in all the world against whom you're holding a grudge, you're out of fellowship with Jesus. Jesus said if you're not willing to forgive your brother his trespasses, neither will your Father in heaven forgive you your trespasses.

James was a rather typical human being. On another occasion James and John, the brothers, came to ask Jesus for the places of highest rank in the kingdom. How characteristic of James's personality. He got angry at the wrong things and he got ambitious in the wrong way. This is an easy pitfall to snare human beings in every generation, but thank God we can see how God's grace changed James.

Let's look now at his—

Purpose.

It may be the historical obscurity of the twelve is due to the fact that their primary purpose was to be witnesses. They were to honor and glorify someone else. They weren't to attract attention to themselves. They weren't to magnify or exalt their own causes or perpetuate their own names. They were there to be witnesses for Jesus.

The natural leaders of the twelve were Peter, Andrew, James, and John. This is supported by the sequence in which these names appear in the Gospels. Of the four, three seemed to have had closest fellowship with Jesus—Peter, James, and John.

They were with him on three significant occasions. Jesus drew them apart after the raising of Jairus' daughter to give them words of special instruction. They were with him at the time of the transfiguration on the mount. Again, at the time of prayer in the Garden of Gethsemane Jesus called three apart, Peter, James, and John. The man whom we study today was one of the inner circle.

There's a strong possibility that James and John were cousins of Jesus on Mary's side. When you take three Gospel accounts, Matthew, Mark, and John, and bring them into focus, you find this possibility. First, in Matthew's Gospel the mother of the two, present at the crucifixion, was called the mother of the sons of Zebedee, James and John. Mark's account does not mention the mother of the sons of Zebedee as one of those surrounding the cross, but it does mention Salome. Hence Salome appears to be the name of the mother of James and John. Finally, John, in his Gospel account, mentions Mary, the mother of Jesus and her sister. He does not mention Salome nor does he mention the mother of the sons of Zebedee. It's entirely likely that one person is designated in these three different ways. This is not a concrete conclusion but a strong possibility.

Reading through the New Testament there are only two sentences ascribed to this James. Because of this, some people say, "Surely he was a shy, reticent person." Yet if Jesus called him a son of thunder it's far more likely that he was a big man in his zeal, in his ambition for the kingdom, and that he possessed a breadth and depth in mind and action.

Let's think now of his—

Persecution.

James was one of those who received the outpouring of the Holy Spirit on the day of Pentecost. As the forward thrust of that great climactic experience was being felt, Peter and John aroused the anger of the Jewish leaders by their preaching. Stephen was stoned to death for his faith. James rose to leadership in the church, and Saul of Tarsus began a systematic persecution of Christians.

When the Jews saw that Christianity continued to spread in spite of all their efforts, they again enlisted the help of the Romans. Herod, who was a Roman official, in A.D. 42 stepped in and killed James, the brother of John, with the sword. He died by decapitation at the hands of a Roman, but the Roman was prompted and pushed into doing this by the ire or wrath of the Jewish leaders.

It's beyond belief that Herod would kill an unknown. If you were to try to stop a movement and knew the way to stop it was by eliminating its leaders, you'd go to the top man, wouldn't you? I have no doubt but that Herod killed the man he thought was the recognized leader in the church—James, brother of John, son of thunder.

If Communists took over in America, past patterns indicate they would begin a systematic elimination of Americans, putting to death up to a third of our population. They would kill or eliminate every community leader and every person with such strong convictions he could not be reeducated and brainwashed to the Communist line. You see, when a shaky new regime like that takes over, the only way it can maintain stability is by eliminating all those who would oppose it. This is the reason Communist-dominated nations have no continued general uprising. All the leaders are killed or imprisoned. All of those with the kind of convictions that would cause them to give their lives for the cause of freedom have been wiped out. When Herod wanted to stop the progress of the Christian faith, he began by killing the outstanding leader.

At the time of his death James was probably in his late thirties or early forties but he proved to us, as Jesus did, that it's not *how long* you live that matters. It's *how* you live that really counts.

The unchanged fact is that Christianity costs. Maybe not your life in martyrdom, but the cost factor is built in. You may not suffer the guillotine or be decapitated for your faith, but the price you pay, though far less colorful, is just as imperative. We're called upon to pay the price of faithfulness, and not too many are willing even to give their time. We must sacrifice selfish wants in order to give our money, but we are largely unwilling to deny ourselves, our lusts and desires for someone or something else. We must attend. We must be faithful, and we must be willing to die for Jesus' sake if called upon. But even more, we must be willing to live for Jesus in the here and now.

The songwriter put it like this:

All on the altar, dear Jesus,
    All at Thy feet I lay,
Willing to toil and to suffer,
    Throughout life's little day.
My all for Thee, my all for Thee,
Who gave Thine all, dear Lord, for me.
    Thy will divine
    Henceforth is mine,
To live for Thee, to live for Thee.

IV
JOHN—BELOVED APOSTLE
Mark 1:19-20

More men bear the name John than any other. There are a number of reasons for this, one of which is family tradition. Many men receive the name from their fathers, and as they look into their family history, perhaps the reason the original John in a certain family was given that name has grown dim. Maybe the name is popular because it's understood that in Hebrew John means "God is gracious." Possibly it's because there have been outstanding men in history who bore the name John that it's given to more male babies than any other name.

It could be the name John is widely used today because John was the apostle whom Jesus loved. I know of no reason Christian parents would prefer to give the name to their son than the fact that John, in the first century, was one whom Jesus loved.

The apostle John was one of the inner circle, composed of Peter, James, and John. They were with our Lord on special, significant occasions. They received particular instructions from the lips of Jesus. Of these three, John was likely closer to Jesus Christ than any other. Now if that's true of the three, the inner circle, it would be even more true of the twelve. It is probable that John was closer to our Lord than any other human being during his earthly sojourn. What an enviable position he held—to walk in closest fellowship with Jesus, the Son of the living God.

The Gospels, at best, have relatively meager accounts of the life of our Lord. There are so many unanswered questions concerning

Jesus and the record of his life on earth. If that's true of Jesus, it's far more true of the twelve apostles, for the biographical material found in the New Testament regarding these men is scanty. There are only two sources of information about Jesus and the twelve. Those are Scripture and tradition.

You can imagine that tradition has become distorted across a period of twenty centuries. When tradition is transmitted orally it can easily become twisted. Fiction can be added to fact in layer after layer, until the germ of truth found at the center of tradition is exceedingly hard to uncover.

One of the traditions about the apostles is that most of them died martyrs' deaths. We have little reason to doubt this, but part of the tradition held that Simon Peter was crucified for his faith with his head downward, rather than in the position in which his Lord was crucified. I know of no reason to doubt such tradition, but there's no authentic base for it. It's word-of-mouth transmission and not substantiated in the original record, the New Testament. So it is with many of the traditional accounts. Some of these can be fitted precisely into the life-style and pattern of Jesus and the twelve, but there is no authority for our saying these are true. When we read the New Testament account, the inspired, infallible word of God, we have every reason to take our stand and say, "This is true; the Bible proclaims it and we believe it."

Leaning most heavily on Scripture today, yet not being unmindful of certain traditions, we'll look first at John's—

Characteristics.

Every personality has distinct characteristics. No two human beings are precisely alike. This is true of you and me. There are things about your life that distinguish you from all other human beings. It was true of John, the apostle.

I feel it's unfortunate that John has been distorted in the pictures artists have painted of him. In some cases an artist's conception of John is that he is a beardless, delicate dreamer. When we think of the pictures painted depicting this apostle whom Jesus loved, it's apparent that he is pictured as being effeminate. Nothing could be farther from the truth! Granted that he was the disciple whom Jesus loved, the picture we get of him in the New Testament is that there was nothing lovable about him. To think that he was effeminate is to stretch the credulity beyond the breaking point.

I lived for seven years on the Gulf of Mexico. There were many fishing boats, shrimpers, and pogy boats that came in and out of the harbor at Gulfport, Mississippi, and Biloxi, the neighboring city. I had occasion to go fishing once in awhile on commercial boats and others. I have never yet seen a man associated with commercial fishing who could be construed as sissy. I have never seen an effeminate person involved in that industry. They are men in the truest sense of the word. They are strong. They are stalwart. They make their living by the strength of their physical bodies. They are not sissies. If that's true today it surely was even more true in the day when Jesus lived. These men who were commercial fishermen cannot be looked upon as effete.

John had a hot, startling temper. He was given to terrible outbursts of anger. He probably knew all of the four-letter words common to the Greek language in the first century. He was much like the Sea of Galilee, upon which he was raised and from which he gained his living.

Like his brother James, John was a man of ambition. You'll recall how the two brothers came to Jesus asking for the places of honor in glory. They wanted Jesus to assign them positions on his right hand and on his left when he came into the fullness of his kingdom. I don't know why they possessed that kind of ambition. Some of us are honest enough to admit why we are ambitious in certain ways.

It could be that John was ambitious in this regard because he and his brother James felt they were socially superior to the remainder of the twelve. Did you get that little phrase, almost overlooked, in our text? When Jesus came and called James and John from the boats of their father Zebedee they left him in the boats with "the hired servants." That surely points to a measure of wealth. It indicates a degree of success in their business, for it was not simply a family operation. It was not carried on by Zebedee and his boys, James and John. It was a business of such magnitude that he employed other men to help them carry it out. Obviously they must have had considerable income to permit that.

Could it be that James and John felt that they were economically ahead of the others, and for economic reasons asked Jesus for these places of honor? That certainly is a possibility.

Another possible factor could be their earthly kinship with Jesus. Jesus had an earthly mother and no earthly father. He had a heavenly Father and no heavenly mother. On his earthly mother's side there is the strongest possibility that Mary was a sister of the mother of James and John. If that be true, then after the flesh, James and John were the cousins of Jesus. It may be on the basis of that kinship they came asking for places of distinction and honor in the kingdom. They felt that they ought to have special consideration, and they certainly were not above pulling the strings to get it.

That John had a vile, unstable temper is indicated by the nickname Jesus gave to him and his brother, sons of thunder, Boanerges. Both of these sons of Zebedee had the same type tempers, the same kind of dispositions.

In all the New Testament there is only one occasion where we find John appearing alone. This is in the ninth chapter of the Gospel of Mark, verses 38-40. John had seen another man ministering to a demon-possessed person. This other man had cast out the demon in the name of Jesus. When he looked at this man he didn't recognize him. He'd never seen him before. He'd never been with them when they were following Christ or hearing Christ. He was a total stranger. Do you remember what John did? He told that man to cease and desist. He wanted to know who he thought he was to be casting out demons in the name of Jesus. He ordered him to stop it and stop it now! Could there have been an element of envy or jealousy in that attitude on the part of John? If so, it's not unfamiliar to us today, for that spirit still exists. Most of us are afflicted in some degree with such sins.

The quickest way to draw the ire of others is to do something positive. The only people who are not being subjected to criticism are those doing nothing. As unbelievable as it may seem in the kingdom of God, if a church rouses itself and begins to minister in the name of Jesus, the criticism from other churches and other church members will be directed toward that church. That's far too true to even cause a smile.

A certain church in Texas has a prominent position; it's known across the nation. But in recent years its membership had declined; its fellowship had lost its sparkle, and it seemed there was no future for that once great downtown church. In the calling of a new pastor the church received a real injection of enthusiasm, and the Holy Spirit seemed to take control in a different way. All of a sudden that church which many people had consigned to the graveyard of churches shook itself, dusted itself off, shed its graveclothes, and began to walk in the power of God's Spirit. Whereas the Sunday School had been on the downward side for 20 years, all of a sudden it began to skyrocket. The numbers increased so fantastically that there was no logical explanation other than the power of God.

Then strangely a chorus of criticism began. From every corner people asked, "What's going on down there? What are they doing? How are they doing it?" Someone said, "They are having contests." Another said, "I heard they gave away a bicycle." Can you imagine a Sunday School that had declined to four or five hundred, suddenly jumping up to about 2000 in attendance with thousands of people being saved? This could draw the criticism of Christians? Yes, that's possible, for it's just one of the facts of life. It's as old as the kingdom of God. Even John, our Lord's closest associate on earth, became jealous and angry when he saw a man whom he did not know ministering in the name of Jesus. What tragic intolerance marked his life. We simply must not be guilty of that sin.

After commanding that man to quit what he was doing, John went to report to Jesus what he had discovered. Our Lord commanded John to let him alone, for Jesus said, "He that is not against us is on our part." If a man is ministering in the name of Jesus he's not our enemy, he's our friend. Isn't it sad that Christians oftentimes use up their live ammunition shooting at each other and then try to put out the inferno of hell with water pistols? We've used up all of our ammunition trying to tear down one another, and when we turn to the fight against Satan we've depleted our armory.

These are just some of the characteristics of John. Let's think for a moment of the—

Change

—that took place in his life.

Strong men can make terrible blunders, but strong men are also capable of deep commitment. When did the change take place that transformed John, the son of thunder, into John, the apostle of love? There was a real change, and it obviously traces itself to experiences that John had with Jesus.

Let me name two I believe were transforming. The first of these must have been the Lord's Supper. You see, the apostles were just like us. They were a jealous group, squabbling over who had done the most, who ought to get the credit, who was the most important, and who deserved the greatest reward. In the midst of that kind of appalling behavior Jesus got a basin of water, filled it, and with a towel over his shoulder began to wash and dry their feet. That factious group of apostles saw our Lord performing a menial, unwanted, unpleasant task usually reserved for the humblest slave in the household. The slave who couldn't be depended upon to do anything else, who couldn't cook a decent meal, who couldn't be relied upon to clean the house, who could not be responsible for overseeing the master's land, the one who could do almost nothing, was given the responsibility for washing the feet of guests and wiping the dust and grime of Palestine from their feet.

Jesus took that task on himself. That must have been far beneath
the dignity of that scrapping, divisive bunch of disciples, but it wasn't
beneath the dignity of our Lord, who came not to be ministered
unto but to minister and give his life a ransom for many.

John couldn't have missed the significance of that. He could not
have failed to be impressed by the contrast. Here he was thinking
of a chief seat, the place of honor in glory, of exalting himself and
advancing his own cause. Jesus, in total self-effacement, bent down
and washed the filth off of his feet. That very same night Jesus
said the words found in John 13:34, "A new commandment I give
unto you, that ye love one another." That's the distinguishing mark
of the Christian faith. That's what makes the Christian religion so
vastly different from every other world religion.

We, in the spirit of Jesus, are to love one another. We're not
given the privilege of interpreting how we're to love each other.
Jesus gave the guideline for that. He said, "As I have loved you,
that ye also love one another." Brother, that leaves no room for
the bitterness, the rancor, all of that little spirit which says, "Oh,
I'll forgive him but I won't forget it." There's no room for that
in the life of a child of God. "A new commandment I give unto
you, that ye love one another; as I have loved you, that ye also
love one another."

I think it must have been on that night the cleansing began. That
cleansing removed more than dirt and grime from the feet of John,
the beloved; it removed his arrogance, sinful pride, and ambition.

Another occasion certainly played into the change that took place
in John's life. No one could have witnessed the crucifixion of our
Lord without being changed. I don't know how many of the twelve
were there. I know for sure John was. Could he have witnessed
that scene without his emotions overflowing? Can you stand before
Calvary's scene in your mind's eye and identify Jesus Christ as your
substitute without being emotionally moved? There are many people
who want a religion of intellect, or who want to make the Christian

religion a matter of debate, a matter of intellectual ball-handling, but I can't understand how any human being can think of the cross and Calvary without being moved to the depths of his emotions.

John saw there the truth that "God was in Christ, reconciling the world unto himself." If one of the Roman centurions was moved to say, "Surely this was the Son of God," how could one of the followers of Jesus have been less moved? It was a touching experience when Jesus committed into his care and keeping the responsibility for his mother, the dearest person he knew on earth. That must have had an effect on John, for he began to understand that Jesus trusted him and believed in him.

After the resurrection it's apparent that John was no longer thinking of himself. He was thinking only of Jesus and reflected the change that had taken place in his life.

Let's note his—

Contribution.

The most deeply devotional treatise ever written about our Lord is the Gospel of John. Prior to the year 1800 there was never any question about the authorship, and even today there is little serious doubt that can be raised.

Paul may have been the theologian who gave impetus to the Christian faith and Christian thought through his writings, but John was the deeply spiritual author who wrote, "For God so loved the world that he gave his only begotten Son, that whosoever believeth on him should not perish, but have everlasting life." You see, that came from a pen of a man who was standing there when Jesus gave his life on Calvary's cross.

John was inspired to write about matters that escaped the notice of other Gospel writers such as the new birth, the water of life, the bread of life, the light of the world, the good Shepherd, my Father's house, and the true vine. In addition to the Gospel, he wrote three Johannine epistles and the Revelation. Paul in Galatians 2:4 mentions John as one of the great leaders of the Christian church.

After twenty centuries of weighing his contribution and testing the ministry of this man, he still stands at the very zenith in Christian history through the impact he's made upon humanity.

One other word. Think of the—

Climax

—of the life of this man. Most scholars agree that he lived a long, long time. His death came around the turn of the first century. He died during the reign of the cruel, sadistic Domitian, who was emperor of the Roman Empire. John was exiled to the island of Patmos. Tertullian, Origen, Eusebius, and Jerome are church historians who all bear witness to that fact. But before his death tradition says that he left the isle of Patmos and spent the last period of his life in the city of Ephesus.

The story is told of a little boy who lived in a home where Grandma lived with the family. He was always given the responsibility of carrying Grandma's packages, for, his parents told him, we want to save Grandma's strength. Grandma was given his downstairs bedroom, and he was moved upstairs so they could save Grandma the steps. On every occasion he was enlisted to help Grandma, to help save Grandma's strength.

One day in bewilderment and desperation he looked at his parents and asked, "What are we saving Grandma for?" Maybe that is a question we need to ask ourselves. Suppose medical science can keep you alive while Social Security and your retirement income keep you up. What for? So you can grow old to be an arrogant, conceited, hotheaded, unchanged old son of thunder? Heaven forbid! Jesus Christ never intended you to become entrenched in your selfishness and shortsightedness, in your hatred and animosity toward other people. Jesus intended you, like John, to change and to grow in your likeness of him and in your revelation of his love in a lost world.

When the Apostle John, the battle-scarred old soldier of the cross, weary with life, homesick for heaven, anxious to be again in the unbroken presence of the living Lord, came to the close of the writing of the Revelation, he penned those words called the blessed hope of the Christian faith. I can imagine after writing laboriously, with greatest difficulty, probably in his nineties, John laid down the quill after he had penned the words and then he prayed the prayer, "Even so, come Lord Jesus." That was the climax, that was the apex of his life. He lived in such close proximity with Jesus here on earth, that when the end came, he was living only for that moment when he'd be translated into the presence of the Lord of glory to live with him forever and ever.

In the little devotional book *Open Windows,* an author recalled an experience from his childhood. He was apparently raised on a farm. His father had been gone for a number of days. He and his two brothers were given the responsibilities of the farm. The day his father came home after an extended absence, he recalled the firewood had been cut unwillingly in insufficient amounts and had just been thrown up against the side of the barn. Many of the tools were lying out in the yard. Rope was hanging here and there, and everything was out of place. The whole farm looked unkempt. He related that as they were in the house, they heard his father's footsteps on the porch. Instead of running to meet him with joy and gladness, they hung back with their heads down. They realized they had been unfaithful in the responsibilities he'd left them and now that he was home they were ashamed. They were afraid to stand and look him in the eye.

Will it be like that at the time of the second coming of Christ with you and me? Will we look into the face of our Lord with shame, with downcast eyes, knowing that we've been flagrantly, openly unfaithful? Or will we, with anticipation, like John the beloved apostle, be praying at the moment he comes, "Even so, come Lord Jesus." That was the climax of John's life and it brings us to an opportunity to make a commitment, the commitment that will bring our lives into closest fellowship with our Lord and active service in his kingdom. Who will respond to his call to be witnesses unto him at home and to the ends of the earth?

V
DOUBTING THOMAS
John 20:24-25

A number of years ago a man in a small, private airplane made a highly dangerous and unauthorized flight across the Atlantic Ocean to Europe. When he landed, he was questioned closely by authorities and newsmen. His story was that he'd become confused, and he'd lost his direction. He said in reality he never intended to leave the United States of America. Whether or not his story can be substantiated in fact, he was given the nickname "Wrong-way Corrigan." We've seen references to him periodically ever since.

In January of 1929 Georgia Tech played Cal Tech in the Rose Bowl. At the opening kickoff Cal Tech kicked to Georgia Tech. One of the backs received the kickoff, but when he was tackled, the ball squirted out of his hands into the hands of the waiting Cal Tech center, Roy Riegals. Being unaccustomed to running the football, he circled momentarily and then took off as hard as he could go—in the wrong direction. He had gained 63 yards before being tackled by one of his own teammates. He was given the name "Wrong-way Riegals," and that nickname stuck.

Sometimes nicknames are easier to acquire than they are to overcome. Sometimes we get a nickname early in life and carry it all through our days. For instance, you may know a man whose nickname is "Skinny" who is no longer skinny. There may be a fellow whose nickname was given him when he was heavyset who is no longer heavyset. Nicknames are easy to acquire, but they are hard to shake later in life.

We're studying a man today who has been given the nickname "Doubting Thomas." The fact is most Christians, in our study of the word of God, have discovered that calling this man Doubting Thomas is only a partial truth. In actuality he was one of the most loyal and dedicated of the twelve apostles. We shall see in our study that he was even willing to lay down his life, to die with Jesus Christ. That certainly doesn't sound much like a man who was beset with doubts or who might have succumbed to his doubts.

Let's begin at the beginning. Let's look at his—

Doubts.

Thomas was the kind of man who could not live with an unasked question. The art of gaining and communicating knowledge consists in asking the right kind of questions. That's precisely what Thomas did.

One illustration of this is found in the fourteenth chapter of John. Jesus was talking primarily with the twelve and said, "Let not your heart be troubled: ye believe in God, believe also in me. In my Father's house are many mansions: if it were not so, I would have told you." Now friend, if you are involved in a search for truth, you'd better start with Jesus Christ, for everything he told us is true. He said, "If it were not so," that is, if it were not true, "I would have told you." The quest for the historical Jesus and the Christ of human experience is a quest for truth. No man really finds truth unless or until he finds Jesus, the Son of God.

As he continued Jesus said, "I go to prepare a place for you. And if I go and prepare a place for you, I will come again, and receive you unto myself; that where I am, there ye may be also. And whither I go ye know, and the way ye know." Thomas was the one who immediately responded, "Lord, we know not whither thou goest; and how can we know the way?" I expect the truth is he was expressing the same thing felt in the heart of every other apostle.

Have you ever had a question in your mind and been afraid to ask it? If so, as you sat there in your dilemma someone else may have asked it for you and you were relieved when it was asked and answered. That's happened many times. I believe Thomas was merely the spokesman for the twelve when he said they didn't know where he was going and could not know the way. Thank God that question was not only asked, but answered. Thomas was answered by our Lord when he said, "I am the way, the truth, and the life: no man cometh unto the Father but by me."

Listen to me, friend, I don't care whether you're a Baptist, a Methodist, a Presbyterian, a Roman Catholic, a Campbellite or any other, no man comes to the Father but by Jesus. Our Lord stated it! In answering the question of Thomas he did not respond by saying, "You've got to join the church." He didn't say, "You've got to be baptized." He didn't say, "You've got to take the Lord's Supper." He didn't say you've got to do anything other than come to him. "No man cometh unto the Father, but by me." What a wonderful affirmation that is.

When people ask theological questions the answer most of the time is not found in some high-sounding subject for debate. The answer is to be found in a personal encounter with the living Christ. Jesus didn't point to a theological supposition, he pointed to himself, "I am the Way." If you know me, Jesus implied, you know the way.

The classic passage in the New Testament from which Thomas got his nickname concerns the appearance of Jesus after the resurrection. In order to get this picture pieced together fully, we have to take the various Gospel accounts and bring them into focus. For instance, in Mark's Gospel Jesus Christ, after coming forth from the tomb of Joseph of Arimathea, alive forevermore, appeared first to Mary Magdalene (Mark 16:9). After Jesus revealed himself to Mary Magdalene, she immediately searched out the eleven and said she had seen the living Lord, the one whom the Romans had put to death. The one whom the Jews thought they had removed from the contemporary scene was not dead, but alive! Do you remember the response of the apostles recorded in the Gospel of Mark? They "believed not." That wasn't only Thomas. That was the entire band of apostles.

In another passage Jesus appeared next to two of the apostles as they were walking in the country and those two, when they returned from that walk, searched out the others and told them whom they had seen. And the text said, "They yet believed not" (Luke 24:41).

In another appearance Jesus, alive after his crucifixion and burial, appeared to the apostles who had gathered in a room where they were weeping and bemoaning his death. In Mark 16:14 we have this account: "Afterward he appeared unto the eleven as they sat at meat, and upbraided them with their unbelief and hardness of heart, because they believed not them which had seen him after he was risen." We call Thomas "Doubting Thomas," but we could also call Simon Peter "Doubting Simon." We could call Andrew "Doubting Andrew," we could call John "Doubting John." Every one of them doubted until they saw Jesus Christ.

Thomas, of course, missed that resurrection rally on the first Easter Sunday morning. When the others reported to him that they had seen Jesus and he was alive, he said he was not going to believe until he could see for himself. They had seen for themselves and they believed on the basis of experience. Thomas said he would believe on the same basis. Though he bears the nickname, Thomas was actually no more incredulous and unbelieving than any of the rest.

Turning from his doubts, let me underscore his—

Devotion.

Thomas was a man of real courage. His first appearance in the New Testament occurs in the Lazarus experience recorded in the eleventh chapter of John. There we remember that word reached Jesus and the apostles that Lazarus was on his deathbed. He was critically ill. When Jesus got that bad news he stayed where he was, continuing his ministry for two whole days. Some couldn't understand this. Mary and Martha, the sisters of Lazarus, couldn't understand it. Why didn't Jesus go immediately? They told him of the illness of his dear friend and Jesus did nothing at all.

Now keep this in mind. The ministry of our Lord had aroused great animosity on the part of the religious leaders in Jerusalem. They were out to get him, and on at least two occasions prior to the Lazarus experience, they had threatened him with stoning. Every time they found him, every time they saw him, his life was in jeopardy. Any time he was found in Jerusalem he was subject to persecution, to threats, or even death. In order for Jesus to get from the place where he was ministering to the home of Lazarus in Bethany, it was necessary to go through Jerusalem. Bethany is a little community about four miles out of Jerusalem. Today travelers to Israel are shown a cave said to be the tomb where Lazarus actually was buried and from which the voice of God called him back into life and physical health.

Jesus announced to the twelve that Lazarus was dead and then said to them, "Let us go into Judea again." Every one of the twelve knew he had to go through Jerusalem. They knew the problem that faced them there. They understood the possibility of persecution and death. It was Thomas who responded, "Let us also go, that we may die with him." They felt sure that if Jesus were found going through Jerusalem, he was going to be killed on the spot. There was no doubt in their minds about it. Thomas expressed what every one of them felt. He could see nothing ahead but death, but he was grimly determined to follow Jesus Christ even if it cost him his life. Now the fact that it did not cost him his life in no way diminishes his courage. He was willing to die.

Since the days of World War II there has been a group of men in our military services who are experts at defusing nuclear devices, bombs, land mines, and things of the like. These experts have been called upon any number of times to perform such tasks. As far as I know no one of these men has ever lost his life defusing an unexploded nuclear device.

A man known and loved by all of us, who was a deacon in our church, was one such person. Off of the shore of Spain, a United States military plane went down. It had on board a nuclear device, and men were sent there and defused it. They were not killed because the bomb did not go off, but their lack of personal injury does not detract from their bravery. They were risking their lives to deal with that device. They are brave men. Thank God, they performed their duty without personal injury.

The danger that faced Thomas and that faces these men in the military is not imaginary but real. The danger in going through Jerusalem was real. They could have been killed. They weren't, and we're grateful for it, but Thomas was willing to lay down his life with, and for, Jesus Christ. Doubting Thomas. His doubts surely were resolved, because he was a man of courage.

A man will hardly give his life for a lie. I don't know any human being that would be willing to sacrifice his life to perpetuate a lie. But every one of these apostles ultimately gave his life to perpetuate the truth that they had come to know in Jesus Christ. Thomas was so convinced of the identity of Jesus even prior to the resurrection that he was willing to die for, and with, our Lord. The courage of Thomas is a tribute to his devotion to Jesus.

Let me now point to his—

Discovery.

The risen Lord ultimately appeared to Thomas and banished all of his doubts and uncertainties. Thomas made the highest possible confession, "My Lord and my God." We talk about the great confession of Simon Peter. He, in talking with Jesus Christ said, "Thou art the Christ, the Son of the living God." That's the loftiest theological concept to be found in the Christian faith. Jesus is God incarnate. Simon Peter recognized him as such, but from the standpoint of one's personal relationship with our Lord there is no higher confession than that of Thomas. Using the personal pronoun, sharing his own conviction and his own faith, Thomas said, "My Lord and My God." It's one thing to say, "The Lord and the God," it's something else to say, "A Lord and a God," but it is a saving faith when one can say of Jesus Christ, "My Lord and my God." That's the foundation upon which the Christian life and testimony is built.

When Thomas came to Jesus wanting to put his fingers in the nail prints, wanting to thrust his hand into the spear scar left in his side, Jesus didn't condemn him, he didn't laugh at him. He didn't say, "Thomas, you are being ridiculous and absurd." He invited him to come and do precisely that.

Maybe the reason Jesus didn't condemn Thomas is because doubts are so human. There isn't a one of us who is a Christian but who at some point in his life has experienced doubts and uncertainties. Our Lord also knew that those who struggle through the wilderness of uncertainty ordinarily come out stronger persons in their faith and beliefs. Maybe that's why Jesus didn't condemn Thomas nor refuse him the privilege of actually feeling those wounds himself.

When your doubts come, keep in mind that they are a mixture of belief and unbelief. That's what makes for doubt. There are certain things that you know to be true, then Satan comes and sows the tares among the wheat and he makes us uncertain about our certainties. I believe when that moment comes it's necessary for Christians to continuously doubt their doubts and believe their beliefs! Those things you have come to know are true must be reaffirmed, and we must put a question mark over the doubts that have made our minds question.

The discovery Thomas made was not based on intellect alone. His discovery was based upon a personal encounter with the living Christ. Your doubts will be resolved and dissolved in the same way. It's not just intellectual assurance you need, it's a personal experience with Jesus, the living Lord. Only in that way can one ever know the reality of salvation.

Remember that Thomas made his discovery in the company of believers. It's far more likely that you'll recognize who Jesus is if you're among Christians than when you're with pagans or even by yourself. I have a real suspicion of those who say that they can get closer to God out fishing or on the golf course than they can in the company of the believers. I have a question mark about people like that. I just don't believe it, for that's not the way God intended it. That's not the way Jesus set up his kingdom. Jesus didn't set up his kingdom for all of us to be little "Lone Ranger" Christians, everyone off by himself, worshiping God the way he sees fit. Jesus Christ set it up for his followers to be a part of the company of believers and unitedly to spread the gospel to the ends of the earth.

It's a paradox in our times that we have afforded authority to nonauthorities. Look at the advertising being done on radio and television. If a manufacturing company wants to sell razor blades, who do they get to advertise them? The star quarterback, the league's leading rusher at halfback, or the home-run hitter. Now what does an athlete know about shaving other than his own face? If you want an authority on shaving, why don't you get that authority from a barber? He's the man who shaves a lot of people and he's the man with greater knowledge and experience. If a fellow makes a name for himself in the world of athletics, we look upon him as an authority on any subject: razor blades, beer, whatnot. What a strange age in which we live.

We give authority to celibates in matters pertaining to marriage. Bachelors give instructions concerning happy homes. Individuals whose marriages have failed, or are failing, are the ones who write articles for the paper and books telling everybody how to get along in marriage. We assign authority to nonauthorities.

Persons who have no vital, exciting church life tell those of us who do have an exciting, vital church life what's wrong with our churches. These self-styled authorities whose own interpersonal relationships may well be in disarray are trying to tell others of us how to live the Spirit-filled life.

I never cease to be amazed at those individuals whose churches are dying and whose spiritual lives are dried up and atrophied, trying to tell Baptists "how to do it." On every hand these nonauthorities speak with great authority. My friend, it may well be that your doubt comes from that source. Maybe you are listening to a nonauthority parading under the guise of authority.

I want you to know the way to resolve your doubts is through a personal, continuing walk with Jesus Christ. He's the only authority on life. He's the only authority on death. He's the only person who ever experienced both and lived to tell us what it's all about. If you want to hear something from an authority, turn to him—he, who knows our tomorrows, who knows the end from the beginning, who holds the whole world in his hands.

I want to remind you that the way to get power with God is the way to power with, and in, Jesus Christ. The power of God is the power of Jesus Christ. The power of the Holy Spirit is the power of the living Christ. You don't have the power of God if you don't have Jesus in your heart. If you say that you have the love of God and the love of the Holy Spirit, you haven't got either one if you haven't got Jesus. He's the one. He's the center and the circumference of it all, and I'm here to remind all of us that our doubts oftentimes are unresolved simply because of our rejection of the revealed Word of God. In God's Word, the answer is repentance and faith regarding man's one universal problem. The problem is sin, and it requires repentance toward sin and faith in the Lord Jesus Christ for that problem to be eliminated.

Talk to an authority. Talk to someone who knows Jesus Christ. Talk to someone who walks daily with Jesus Christ. Talk to someone to whom Christ has revealed himself and in whom Jesus Christ lives. You'll be talking to an authority whom you can trust and whose testimony you can believe.

VI
NATHANAEL BARTHOLOMEW
John 1:45-51

As we come to this point in our study of the twelve apostles, we confront for the first time a problem of identification. It centers in the fact that in four places in the New Testament the name Bartholomew is found in the list of the twelve apostles. These four appearances are in Matthew 10:3; Mark 3:18; Luke 6:14; and Acts 1:13. By comparison, the other Gospel writer, the apostle John, never lists Bartholomew but names Nathanael. I believe there are adequate reasons for equating these two. I believe they are one and the same man.

The name Bartholomew is a patronymic, that is, a family name. In the study of another apostle, Simon Peter, we learned that he was Simon Bar-jona. The prefix "bar" means "son of." Bartholomew then means "son of Talmai" or perhaps "Tolmai." Consequently this was not the only name he had. Bar-jona was to be considered the last name of Simon Peter. Jesus gave him a new name, but prior to that his name was Simon Bar-jona. Bartholomew's other name must have been Nathanael, by which he is called in the Gospel of John. Matthew, Mark, and Luke never mention Nathanael. John never mentions Bartholomew. Because of the familiarity these Gospel writers had with the twelve apostles, it stands to reason that these men knew the dual appellations of the twelve and never dreamed there would be any confusion or misunderstanding. When John called him Nathanael, Matthew, Mark, and Luke knew immediately to whom he referred. When Matthew, Mark, and Luke referred to him as Bartholomew, John and the others knew the one to whom he was referring. So we bring those names into equation, believing them to refer to one man.

Another reason for believing this identification to be true is that it's hardly possible John would have given this much attention to the conversion of a man who did not have great importance in the New Testament church. John describes in detail the conversion of Nathanael. Had he been relatively unknown in the Christian community, it's not likely John would have related this experience so fully.

I find a number of things in these brief verses I believe are important. Let's underscore Nathanael's—

Perplexity.

When Philip found Nathanael, and obviously he was looking for him, he invited him to come to Jesus. When Nathanael did, Philip identified Jesus as the one of whom Moses and the prophets had written. Jesus called Nathanael "an Israelite indeed." In other words, he was a true son of Abraham. He was a Hebrew of the Hebrews. He doubtless had great familiarity with the teachings of the Old Testament. He knew when Philip said, "We have found him, of whom Moses in the law, and the prophets did write," that he was describing the Messiah, the Promised One, the Holy One of Israel, God's Son. There was no problem there insofar as Philip's introduction was concerned.

I believe Philip is a man who needs to be studied and whose pattern needs to be followed today. He illustrates the fact that a person either ought to give away his faith or he ought to give it up. If you've got living faith in the living Christ, you ought to be sharing that faith with other people. If your faith is well founded, if you have in your heart the joy of salvation, you ought to be telling other people.

Did you notice in these verses, beginning with 41, the number of times the verb "found" and "findeth" appear? Four or five times it is recorded. When Andrew "found" Jesus Christ, he turned and "findeth" his brother. When Philip "found" the Messiah, he "findeth" Nathanael. When you and I "find" Jesus Christ in the free pardon of sin, it becomes our solemn and binding duty to "find" others who have never "found" his grace and forgiveness.

When Philip identified Jesus as the one of whom Moses and the prophets wrote, the son of Joseph, immediately Nathanael revealed his perplexity. "Can anything good come out of Nazareth?" he asked. Being familiar with the Old Testament, Nathanael knew that the prophets had predicted Bethlehem to be the birthplace of God's Messiah. An Old Testament writer wrote: "And thou Bethlehem, in the land of Judah, art by no means least among the cities of Judah; for out of thee shall come a ruler who will govern my people Israel."

The perplexity of Nathanael might have been caused by Philip's identification of Jesus as being from Nazareth. Nazareth, of course, was many miles removed from Bethlehem. Nathanael couldn't understand that. If this one is the Messiah, he should be from Bethlehem. Of course Jesus was born in Bethlehem, but he grew up in the home of Joseph and in the carpenter shop in Nazareth and was recognized as a Galilean.

In John 21:2 we learn that Nathanael came from the village of Cana of Galilee. There are some interesting insights here. You remember, of course, that our Lord performed the first miracle of his public ministry at Cana of Galilee. That was the hometown of Nathanael Bartholomew. The little village of Cana and Nazareth, being close by geographically, were familiar with one another and possibly this caused contempt.

We know about community rivalries. Sometimes today those rivalries stem from high school athletics, sometimes from business competition, sometimes it is a result of population or census figures where one city is at first ahead and then the other, and two cities seemingly vie with each other. Often the competition is a result of business indicators, bank deposits, or total sales of the business firms. We're familiar with competition between cities. This was possible between Cana and Nazareth.

It's unfortunate that we often become prejudiced toward those with whom we are in competition. I think, for instance, of the phenomenon that exists in the state of Texas regarding the Texas Aggies. I recall the sentiment on the part of Aggies and others toward the University of Texas, "teasippers" as they are sometimes called. I know that kind of rivalry, and I know some persons who have so closed their minds to graduates of a particular school that they don't think anything good at all can come out of that institution. That kind of prejudice can blind our minds to truth, and I fear that's the kind of prejudice Nathanael had when he responded to Philip's invitation as he did, "Can there any good thing come out of Nazareth?"

He had known Nazareth all of his life. He knew a lot about Nazareth, some fact and some fiction, but he had already decided out of contempt for the rival village that nothing good could come out of it.

It was at this point that a great transformation took place in the life of Nathanael. Jesus Christ not only redeemed his soul from hell and assured him of a place in heaven, but he purged his heart of that hellish prejudice which was revealed in the conversation with Philip.

Many years ago the Wright brothers were building the first airplane on the sand dunes of Kitty Hawk, North Carolina. Word of their project reached their hometown of Dayton, Ohio. There was one skeptic in Dayton who, having known the Wright brothers all their lives, was heard to say: "No one will ever fly through the air. If anyone ever does, he won't be from Dayton, Ohio. And if anyone from Dayton, Ohio, ever flies through the air, it certainly won't be one of those Wright boys." That fellow was a three-time loser! Someone did fly through the air, he was from Dayton, Ohio, and it was one of the Wright boys!

Jesus said that a prophet is not without honor save in his own country and in his own house. There is a natural, inborn prejudice toward those with whom we are familiar. Sometimes the prejudice is based on petty jealousies, sometimes on rivalry, sometimes on personal animosity, but it's hard to see greatness in the lives of those with whom we are familiar. We find it hard to believe that greatness can spring out of familiar soil. All the really great people are from way off somewhere! All of the true experts are those who live in a distant city. Those closest to home are seldom accorded their true value.

This is part of the perplexity of Nathanael, but I'd like for us to remember the—

Praise

—Jesus heaped upon him. This praise from the lips of Jesus of Nazareth was, "Behold an Israelite indeed, in whom is no guile." This is an amazing characteristic, for guile is defined as deceit, cunning, duplicity, or fraud. Jesus could see none of that in Nathanael. In him there was no guile. In other words, Nathanael was an open man. He was sincere and honest. When he said something, one could believe it. When he took his stand, one could always know where he was. Not the kind of individual who would talk out of both corners of his mouth, he was the man whc would state his position and stand by it.

Maybe you recall the ancient story of a man named Diogenes. He went about in the daytime carrying a lighted lantern. When people would stop him and ask why he did this, his reply was that he was searching for an honest man. That's the kind of man Nathanael was, a man in whom there was no guile.

It seems obvious that these characteristics were as rare in Jesus' day as they are in our own. If everyone was without guile in Jesus' time, he would not have recognized this characteristic as outstanding and worthy of praise. There are not many adults who can say, "I am without guile." There's so much deceit, duplicity, cunning, and fraud in us all that we pause when we read Christ's praise of Nathanael Bartholomew.

Ordinarily one finds this characteristic more frequently in little children than adults. Stop a child and ask him pointed questions, and the chances are he'll give you direct, forthright answers. Ask him, "How do you get along with your brothers and sisters?" and he'll tell you. Ask him, "Do you fight with your other brothers and sisters?" and he'll tell you. Ask him, "Do your mother and father fuss and argue about money?" and he'll tell you. Art Linkletter capitalized on this in a television show that ran for many years, *People Are Funny.* He talked to little children and they would give answers that would curl their parents' hair. The parents couldn't stand it when the children answered honestly every question asked them. We find that trait more frequently in a child than in an adult.

Do you suppose that might have prompted our Lord to say, "Except ye be converted and become as little children, ye shall not enter into the kingdom of heaven"? A little child is honest, he's without guile. He's not trying to prove a point, not trying to keep something hidden, not trying to shade truth with a half-truth; he tells it like it is.

Jesus also said to let your yea be yea and your nay nay. That means let your yes mean yes, and when you say no, let it mean no. An honest man never has to add anything to a simple yes or to a straightforward no. When a man says, "I swear I'm telling the truth," one immediately puts a question mark over the veracity of his statement. An honest man has no need to swear. An honest man can say, "This is the way it is," or, "This is the way it was," and people accept his word. For a liar, a man whose life is marked by guile, there are no adjectives adequate to make his word valid. All of the cursing in the world, all of the swearing one may do cannot make an honest man out of a liar. If one tells the truth, it needs no embellishment. If he does not, nothing he says can twist it around and make it true. Let your yea be yea and your nay nay. Little children are truthful, without guile. Sadly enough there are not many adults deserving of the praise Jesus gave Nathanael Bartholomew.

Little children are not only truthful, they are willing to be shown. Maybe that's another reason Jesus praised Nathanael. When Philip said, "Come and see," Nathanael immediately agreed. He was ready to go and see, and he went. He came face to face with Jesus, the Messiah, the Son of God. Nathanael was willing to be shown. He didn't begin an elaborate debate as to why it was not practical or feasible for him to leave what he was doing to go to Jesus. He didn't try to put it off until a more convenient time. He didn't say: "I'm already occupied now. Can't you see how busy I am?" He was willing to be shown.

That's a prime characteristic in the life of a child. Ask a child if he'd like to go with you to see most anything, and he'll look up with a bright smile, give you his hand, and say, "Let's go."

It occurs to me that any lost man who is not saved, who is not a Christian, cannot be an honest man unless he's willing to be shown. You see, all this information about Jesus may be information you've never had. It may be you're ignorant of it, but if you're honest, you will be willing to accept truth, however it is conveyed to you. Basic honesty requires a lost man to see for himself. If Jesus Christ is who he says he is, then Jesus can do for you what he's done for us. You owe it to yourself, if you are an honest person, to try Jesus at his word. Take his words, apply them to your own life, open your heart in honesty to him, confess your sin, and see if Jesus will do what he said.

Philip said to Nathanael, "Come and see." Nathanael responded immediately and came to Jesus, and the result of his guilelessness was conversion and the call to apostleship. That same thing will be true in the life of any lost person honest enough to take Jesus at his word. If you're not honest enough to open your heart and see what he's willing to do for you, there really is nothing that can be done. Basic honesty. "Behold an Israelite indeed, in whom is no guile."

We see Nathanael's perplexity, we hear the praise Jesus gave him. Now I want to say a word about the—

Promise

—which our Lord made Nathanael.

After Jesus described Nathanael under the fig tree in study and prayer, Nathanael perceived that Jesus had wisdom beyond ordinary humans. When he came to Jesus, our Lord said, "When thou wast under the fig tree, I saw thee." Nathanael was astounded. He was far removed from our Lord, out of eyesight, and there was no way that Jesus could have known other than in the omniscience of God. Jesus knew the whereabouts of Nathanael by divine knowledge.

Jesus Christ knows the whereabouts of every lost person on the face of the earth today and in every generation from the beginning of time. Jesus knows where you are, what shape you're in physically and spiritually, and everything there is to know about you! More than anything else he wants to save you. He wants you to "come and see" for yourself.

When Nathanael perceived who Jesus was, he cried out, "Rabbi, thou art the Son of God; thou art the King of Israel." Do you see the understanding Nathanael possessed? The word "rabbi" is also translated teacher or master. He acknowledged Jesus Christ as "Rabbi," Master. He acknowledged him as "Son of God," that is, Mediator. He is God in human flesh who came to reconcile the world unto himself. Then Nathanael said, "Thou art the King of Israel." In other words, the promised Messiah. He is the one of whom Moses and the other prophets wrote. Nathanael, with a burst of divine insight, grasped the identity of Jesus Christ. He is Master, Mediator, Messiah. He understood and believed because he was willing to come and see for himself.

Jesus made Nathanael a promise. He said, "Thou shalt see greater things than these. . . . Hereafter ye shall see heaven open, and the angels of God ascending and descending upon the Son of man." What a glorious promise that was, and it surely must have whetted the appetite of Nathanael, giving him something toward which to be looking. That promise was fulfilled.

Some commentators see in this promise a reference to Genesis 28:12, which is the vision that Jacob had of the ladder from heaven with the angels ascending and descending, the two-way traffic of heaven. It is possible that on the journey Jesus was making from Judea, where Jerusalem was located, northward into Galilee, they were at the spot geographically that was closely associated with the life of Jacob. It surely was in that neighborhood.

The brook Jabbok, the place called Bethel where the altar was established, and other familiar landmarks lay very close to the route one would ordinarily take going from Jerusalem into Galilee. It may be that they were at that spot when Jesus made the promise to Nathanael. How wonderfully that promise was fulfilled, for Nathanael did come to know of heaven opened and the angels of God ascending and descending upon the Son of man.

The first experience in which this happened was at the time of the baptism of Jesus. Matthew 3:16 says, "The heavens were opened." Again at the time of the temptation of Jesus in the wilderness the "angels came and ministered unto him" (Matt. 4:11). Again on the mount of transfiguration, the face of our Lord shone with the divine effulgence. As the Shekinah glory of God burst through his flesh, heaven was opened and the approval of God was stated as he said, "This is my beloved Son in whom I am well pleased; hear ye him" (Matt. 17:5). Again in the garden of Gethsemane as our Lord was in the throes of the greatest anguish any human has ever known, heaven opened up. and the sustenance and succor of an angel from on high came, giving him strength and help in that moment of need (Luke 22:43). Nathanael truly saw heaven opened in the ministry of God's only begotton son, the Lord Jesus Christ.

I believe we can draw a parallel to our day from this ladder. You see, the ladder is a two-way ladder. The angels of God not only ascend, they descend. I think that can be applied to our lives as our prayers ascend to the throne room of grace when we call upon God in our need. We ask God for his blessings in our witness and then the blessings of God descend upon us. We have a binding obligation to share these blessings with others all about us.

John Wesley once said there's no such thing as a solitary religion. How very true. It's not enough for those blessings to come to our lives. Blessings must be shared with other people as we share our faith. Having been found, find your brother and share the blessings of salvation—at home and to the ends of the earth.

VII
MATTHEW LEVI
Luke 5:27-32

Our text refers to this apostle as Levi. In a society where it was customary for a man to have two names, he was also called Matthew. The name Matthew means "gift of God." It could well be that this latter name is the one given him by our Lord. When Simon was miraculously converted and called from his fishing vessel and nets to follow Jesus, he was given a new name, Peter. It could well be that the name which our Lord gave to Levi was Matthew, which means "gift of God."

The name Levi is found in Mark 2:14 and also in our text in the fifth chapter of Luke. But in the Gospel that bears his name he refers to himself as Matthew (Matt. 9:9).

We find many insights regarding this man from the Gospel which bears his name and also from his occupation. Let us seek to glean those truths and apply them to our lives and experiences.

There's an interesting possibility here I simply must mention. In Mark 2:14 we find that Matthew was the son of Alphaeus. In Matthew 10:3, in the listing of the twelve apostles Matthew names James, often referred to as James the Less, as being "son of Alphaeus." Now assuming that this Alphaeus is one and the same man, this would mean that Matthew had a brother who was also an apostle. We know about Peter and Andrew, James and John, but there is the strong possibility that there was this other set of brothers among the twelve. Matthew Levi and James both are referred to as sons of Alphaeus. There's no way that we can prove this, so I suppose that we'll have to allow it to remain an unexplained mystery until we stand in the presence of our Lord.

I'd like for us to look at the—

Occupation

—of Matthew Levi. The outstanding fact prior to his call to apostleship is that Levi was a tax gatherer. In the New Testament they are universally referred to as publicans. You can understand the mixture of language in that melting pot, that caldron of world civilization called the Middle East. Like a football those nations around the Mediterranean Sea were bounced back and forth from one aggressor nation or empire to another. One group would become strong militarily and would conquer that part of the world. Then another nation would become strong and would push back the occupying forces and conquer the Middle East.

Palestine had fallen to the kingdom or empire of Alexander and following that came the Roman Empire. The language of the Alexandrian Empire was Greek. The language of the Roman Empire was Latin. You can see the influence of both in the lives of people in the days in which Jesus lived.

The word "publican" comes from the Latin *publicanus.* It meant a public servant but referred primarily to tax collection. Keep in mind that a great highway led from Babylon, down in Egypt, all the way around the fertile crescent, encompassing the Mediterranean seacoast, on into the western part of the Mediterranean world. This highway had a branch that ran up through northern Galilee around the Sea of Galilee. It's on the shores of the Sea of Galilee that the ancient city of Capernaum was located. Visitors to the Middle East today visit the ruins of Capernaum.

One of the positive proofs of the divinity of Jesus Christ and his omniscience is that our Lord predicted that Capernaum would be brought low. Visitors to the Middle East can testify that there is hardly one stone standing upon another in the archaeological excavations of the ancient city of Capernaum. There is a long pier stretching out from those ruins into the Sea of Galilee. Tourist boats pull up there and unload visitors by the scores. The tourists wander across those ruins of a city once great about which Jesus Christ said, "And thou Capernaum . . . shalt be brought down to hell" (Matt. 11:23). Capernaum was.

It was in a little suburb of Capernaum called Bethsaida that Peter and other fishermen lived. This was a very vital, interesting locality during the ministry of Jesus. The great road ran through Capernaum and it was precisely there that Matthew established his tax collection office. What an ingenious place to locate! He was there to observe every fishing vessel that came in with its catch of fish, and in the interests of Roman government he could tax each catch.

Not only that, the travelers of the world passed through Capernaum making their way around the fertile crescent into Greece. It was an ideal location for a tax gatherer. With the full authority of Rome, he collected from everyone who passed.

He could set the taxes himself, for Rome merely required a percentage. Beyond that percentage he could garner anything the traffic would bear. If the tax gatherer looked at you, decided that you were affluent and likely had a great deal of money with you, he could tax you in any way he desired in the proportion he might determine. Imagine how corrupted these individuals became as a result of selfishness and greed. Whatever he could get beyond Rome's percentage he could keep.

Here was a Jew working for Rome, the ruling nation. He was considered by his fellow Jews a traitor to his homeland and his countrymen. Not only that, when he exacted taxes he had the full authority of the Roman soldiers behind him. If someone protested, all this Jewish tax collector had to do was beckon a nearby Roman legionnaire to enforce his decree.

Rome built great roads all over her empire. Some of those roads are still being used today. A visitor to the city of Rome will be shown an aqueduct, built during the days of the Roman Empire, still transporting water into the city of Rome. This was the general time when Jesus, our Lord, was here on earth.

Not only did Rome build great roads but she stationed her soldiers over her empire to guarantee safety and protection to travelers. You might imagine there were thieves and robbers to prey on innocent travelers and oftentimes the robbers were well rewarded for their thievery. The Roman legionnaires were there to guarantee safety, however, and there certainly was a company of Roman soldiers stationed in or near Capernaum.

It was necessary for Rome to tax her subjects in order to support the military budget of the Roman Empire. Every great conquering empire has had a tremendous military budget.

I think it's of more than passing significance that our Lord said those who live by the sword will also die by the sword. It has been true throughout history. Nations that have risen to positions of ascendency and dominance on the basis of their military might have one day encountered another nation with greater military might, and have fallen. It was true of Rome, and will likely be true here in the United States. With a large percentage of tax dollars going to support the military through the programs of the Pentagon, some of which might be absolutely essential and some of which might not be, we find the burden of taxation primarily centered in the military and defense. The same thing was true in Matthew's day. Rome needed tax money to support the armies of Rome around her empire.

Most of the publicans, working in coalition with Rome, were cunning and unjust. They were shrewd, they were able to evaluate an individual at a glance, and they assessed taxes that often were impossible to pay. Then in their craftiness, they would turn around and lend money at an exorbitantly high interest rate to the person being assessed.

A publican usually got his job at a public auction. The job of being tax collector was open for bids. The highest bidder secured the position. But after a man had sold his conscience and sold out his fellow countrymen, it became an easy matter for graft, fraud, greed, and extortion literally to cover him up in unbelievable corruption.

Because he was dealing with travelers from around the world, a publican had to speak a number of languages. We don't know how many languages Matthew Levi spoke, but it could well be that he had the command of four or five different ones. Consequently, he was not only a wealthy individual, he was considered an educated person.

Turning from his occupation, let's remember his life marked by—

Ostracism.

No category of human beings in the ancient world was more hated than tax gatherers. The strict Jew believed it was not right to pay taxes to anyone save God alone. In the common parlance of that day and time, murderers, robbers, and tax gatherers were mentioned in the same breath. Can you see the kind of company they were associated with? Murderers, robbers, and tax gatherers. In the New Testament the words "publican" and "sinner" are most often found in close association.

A tax collector, or publican, was barred from being a witness in any legal trial. He was forbidden to be a judge and was excluded from all services of public worship.

This fact is pointed out in a parable Jesus told, the parable of the Pharisee and the publican. The Pharisee was down close to the front. You see, he was one of the religious elite, a leader of religion in his day. He was down where the action was in the Temple. But the publican, by contrast, stood afar off. He was not permitted to come into the place where the religious leaders could hold forth in their so-called worship. This is one of the most tragic pictures I know. The tragedy is that it has been repeated in our very day.

In that time, just as in our own, those who were regular in worship would look around, nudge one another, and say as they glanced down their pharisaical noses: "Did you see who just walked in? Well, look out, the chandeliers are going to fall." Isn't that a travesty on the gospel of Jesus Christ? If a sinner can't come to the house of God, where can he go? There's no place for him if he can't come to worship. The house of worship is the place where God offers every man a welcome, even you. When I point my index finger at you I've got three coming back at me, and I'm talking about myself. If a sinner can't worship, I can't worship, because I'm a sinner.

But the religious people in Jesus' day, just like religious people in our day, thought they were the only ones who could worship. Now this tax gatherer can't come "in here," this is where God's people meet! The fact of the matter is, if we're God's people we'll understand our obligation to that sinner. He's having a pretty tough time and his heart may be hungry. It could well be that we've got the message he's seeking. If he can't come "in here" and get it, where can he go?

Jesus described the plight of the publican. He had to stand afar off. The Pharisee, who was the religious leader, got on the inside. He was supposed to have direct access to God in his prayer, but his prayer never got as high as the chandelier because he was praying "with himself." He wasn't talking with God. The text said he prayed thus with himself, "God, I thank thee, that I am not as other men." Have you ever felt that way? Think about the poor guys like Matthew Levi, who have hungry hearts, who more than anything else want that peace of God that passeth understanding. How pharisaical we are when we kick them in the teeth and condemn them as they come into the house of God for worship.

The authority of Matthew was obvious. He represented Rome, and his word was law. All people who possessed taxable items showed him great respect. But the religious people passed him by on the other side of the street and would scarcely look in his direction.

Isn't it strange how youngsters frequently reveal parental attitudes? If there is another adult with whom you are at odds, notice the coolness of that person's children toward you. If you have a disagreement with some other adult, you'll see it reflected in his children. They hear their parents talk and adopt the same attitude as their parents. This was true in Jesus' day. I'm confident the youngsters of parents who hated publicans would throw rocks at a publican and then run. Maybe they would seek to get close enough to him, if they were brave, and spit on his clothing and then dash off before being caught. That's the sort of environment in which Matthew lived.

Undoubtedly he had more money than he could spend. But to his surprise, his affluence didn't bring him satisfaction. He found that money couldn't buy everything. No human ever stopped to engage him in conversation, nobody ever asked his opinion, no one ever stopped just to pass the time of day. Childhood friends and associates with whom he had grown up, whom he'd known all his life, wouldn't even speak to him.

I can imagine his wife felt the pinch of ostracism. His wife was unhappy about it, too. I can think of nothing more terrible than having to live with an unhappy woman. Friend, if you've got a wife that doesn't like your occupation, and you're living with her unhappiness while she wallows in her self-pity, then we all ought to be praying for you.

Now here was Mrs. Matthew. She thought when she got enough money to buy all the clothes she wanted, everything would be all right. She had the money, she bought the clothes, but she was denied access to the synagogue where she could show them off. I got news for you fellows! If you haven't figured this out, your wife doesn't want to buy those new clothes just to hang them in the closet or to wear around the house. She wants to buy new clothes to wear where people are. That's just the way things are.

I am sure the same is true with men. When you buy a new suit you don't buy it to work in the yard. You don't buy a new suit to take hunting or fishing. You wear it where the people are, where you'll see the most people.

Mrs. Matthew had a closet full of clothes, but she didn't have anywhere to go to wear them. I expect she was unhappy. She had all the money she needed to hire servants. She had a house full of servants to do her every bidding, but they simply afforded her more leisure time, and her leisure enlarged her loneliness. She sat there and became more and more depressed. Maybe she did as some women in that condition today and turned to alcohol. That's where the alcoholic wives come from. Not from the poor families, but from the families that have reached affluence and can afford to buy the booze. They can afford to drink it, and they've got plenty of leisure time. There comes the problem.

Look at the—

Obedience

—of Matthew. Jesus simply said to him, "Follow me." Matthew had no idea what was required, but at this point in life it didn't make any difference. He was ready for any kind of help from any place where help was offered. Now friend, when a person comes to that point in life, he's ready to get what Jesus offers. As long as you think there's something you can do, some work that you can accomplish, some deed that you can do to guarantee you acceptance before God, the chances are you are going to try to do it your way. But when you come to that point in life when you understand that there's nothing you can do, there is no help that can come to you from any other quarter, and you turn to Jesus Christ, then you are in a position to receive what he has to offer.

It's a tribute to divine wisdom that Jesus saw beyond what Matthew was to what Matthew could be. You can't think of a more unlikely man to be an apostle than Matthew. He was universally hated, he was lost to shame and lost to honor, yet Jesus chose him! Most of us would say that's about as poor public relations as could be. After all, there were men from good backgrounds, men who had all the credentials, who could have been chosen.

I've satisfied my own mind on that problem. The reason Jesus chose Matthew is the same reason he chose me. He didn't come to win a popularity contest. He came to show what God can do with an unlikely person. That's the reason he saved you, and the same purpose still holds.

Luke says when Matthew responded to Jesus' call that he left all and followed him. There's a sense in which he left all, but there's another sense in which he didn't. Thank God he didn't leave his mind and his ability to write down things in an orderly fashion. Thank God he didn't leave his quill and his ability to write behind, because those very talents were utilized in writing down the God-ordained, inspired gospel of Jesus Christ. Can you imagine Jesus picking a man like that? Then can you imagine God using a man like that to put into writing the inspired gospel of God and his eternal purpose? My friend, if God can use Matthew, he can use any man on the face of the earth who has a hungry heart and is willing to be obedient!

Matthew learned the hard way, but he learned well that his purpose in life was not to make a profit for himself. His purpose in life was to make a profit for Jesus Christ. It's significant that his Gospel contains more of the teachings of Jesus than any other book in the New Testament. It was Matthew who remembered and wrote down in order the teachings from the lips of our Lord that we call the Sermon on the Mount, probably the most important Christian teachings in the gospel.

One other word. Let me make some—

Observations.

The first one is, it's a very difficult thing for self-righteous people to understand God's love for sinners. If we can't understand why God loves certain people, we fall into the category of the self-righteous.

Having been born again, Matthew gave a dinner party for the people who were occupied with tax collecting, other outcasts from society. That wasn't a skid row banquet, it wasn't a soup line, it was a banquet at the Woman's Forum for the Country Club set. They came, and Jesus preached to them. But the religious folks couldn't understand it. They criticized Jesus. They thought: Look at him. He's out there fraternizing with those publicans and sinners. What does he want to run around with that crowd for? Why isn't he down here with religious people? Jesus gave the answer, "They that be whole need not a physician."

Who are the folks with the greatest responsiveness? They are not the people who think they've got it made religiously. They are the people who know who they are and what their need is.

To Matthew Levi privilege meant responsibility. Jesus Christ never saved a person without a purpose, and he never saved an individual without having a place of service for that individual to fill. Before his call, Matthew was out with people at the gate of customs, where the action was. After Jesus called him, he was still out there. Not a recluse, not hibernating in an office behind closed doors, but where the people were. He went out in obedience to the command of Jesus Christ.

Matthew was a straight talker. Some people don't like that. Some people don't want a preacher to tell it like it is. Some try always to get one to water it down a little bit and make it more palatable. Matthew was not that kind of man. He recorded some teachings from the lips of Jesus that escaped the notice of other Gospel writers, but they were teachings that meant a great deal to him. Matthew is the one who remembered that Jesus said, "You can't serve God and mammon." To whom could that have been more meaningful? He'd spent a long time trying to serve mammon, but he found he couldn't. He couldn't serve mammon and God.

Matthew is the one who remembered that Jesus said: "But seek ye first the kingdom of God, and his righteousness; and all these things shall be added unto you." To whom could that have meant more and in whose mind could that have stuck with greater tenacity than in the mind of Matthew? Of course Jesus said it, and of course Matthew knew exactly what he was talking about. You can't put money and the things money buys first and have Jesus first. There can't be but one first.

Jesus took this gatherer of taxes and transformed him into a giant for God. That same miracle of grace is being performed today, dear friend. I don't care who you are, or how deeply into sin you may have sunk, or how black your life may be with iniquity, Jesus Christ can perform in your heart the same kind of miracle he performed for Matthew Levi. The requisite is to be obedient. You've got to realize your need, forsake all, and follow him. If you are willing to do that, you have an opportunity now to receive Jesus.

VIII
SIMON THE ZEALOT
Matthew 10:4

The only mention of this man Simon the Zealot in the New Testament is the listing of his name in the Gospels and Acts. Even his name presents a problem, for in Matthew 10:4 and Mark 3:18 he is called Simon the Canaanite. In Luke 6:15 and Acts 1:13 he is called Simon Zelotes. Now for a person reading the New Testament for the first time, it might seem that these are different men. Yet with an understanding of the language and an investigation of the names Canaanite and Zelotes we find the answer.

When we turn to a standard Greek lexicon, Thayer's, we learn that the word translated Canaanite is a Hebrew derivative of the same word from which we get Zelotes. So the two words actually mean one and the same thing. The name given to the party to which Simon belonged is Zealot, hence Simon the Zealot. That one bit of understanding gives us the key that unlocks a vast storehouse of information about the man and the political-religious party to which he belonged.

Let's refresh our minds with the—

Context

—of the times of this man and the life he lived.

Palestine was a subject country. It was under Roman rule, but many Jews never accepted the yoke of bondage. The Hebrew people have always been freedom loving. This is probably a result of their relationship with God and the knowledge that the one true God intended man to be free. Through all the centuries of her existence, Israel has fought for freedom, though she has often been in bondage.

Years before the coming of Christ there was a Roman emperor named Antiochus Epiphanes who perpetrated many unspeakable atrocities against the Jews. One of the things he proposed was designed to be the ultimate insult. This was the worst thing he could think of to do to the Jewish people. He announced publicly that he intended to slaughter a hog on the altar in the holy of holies at the Temple in Jerusalem.

Bring to mind your knowledge of Old Testament history and something of your knowledge of the Temple. In the Temple there was a place called the holy of holies that was entered by only one person, and he only once a year. On the Day of Atonement the high priest went into the holy of holies to offer the sacrifice for the sins of the people. It was probably the most sacred spot to the Jewish people in all the earth. When Antiochus Epiphanes, the Roman emperor, said he was going to sacrifice a hog in the holy of holies, he was desecrating everything the Jews held dear.

You know even today the attitude of strict Jews toward pork. They will not eat it. They looked upon swine as unclean and defiling. They would not touch pork as food and would have no contact with swine. To sacrifice a hog in the holy of holies was the worst thing Antiochus could do to the Jewish people. You can get some idea now of the proportion of the insult that he intended.

At the time of the reign of Antiochus Epiphanes, there rose to prominence a Jewish family called the Maccabees. These men were freedom fighters. They were leaders of the opposition against Rome and were folk heroes among the Jews. The father of the Maccabees, named Mattathias, made this statement when dying: "And now, my children, be zealous for the law and give your lives for the covenant of your fathers." That dying wish from the lips of Mattathias formed the source of the name for this political-religious party called the Zealots. He urged his son to be zealous. The Zealots, then, were those who were zealous for the law and for the covenant of their fathers.

The Zealots were the last great Jewish party to emerge and they trace their origin to the Maccabees and opposition to Roman rule. They were the most fervently patriotic of all the Jews. Their battle cry was, "For God and country." There have been untold thousands of patriots from that day to this who have given their lives with that same cry, under the same banner, "For God and country."

The Zealots envisioned Israel as a theocracy. You see the dependence that we have in English upon Greek. The word "theocracy" means "the rule of God," *theos* meaning "God." Our word "theology" means "a study of God." Our word "democracy" comes from the Greek word *demos* which means "people," therefore "a rule of people." A monarchy is the rule of one man. So the Zealots looked upon Israel as a theocracy. They felt a responsibility only to God, his commands were the only ones to be obeyed, and any who sought to bring them into bondage was to be resisted.

For the strict Jew, God was the only king, therefore, the rebellion of the Zealots against Rome was not considered a political insurrection, but a holy war. Men give themselves in fanatical zeal for a war that appeals to their religious beliefs. Such was the party of the Zealots. The apostle Simon the Zealot was a former member of that party.

Think with me of some of the—

Conditions

—that prevailed in Palestine in that day.

This little land was composed of a number of clearly defined regions. Israel, in our generation, is so defined from a topographical point of view. The fighting taking place on the southern borders of Israel is being waged in the Sinai Peninsula. At the extremity of that peninsula runs the Suez Canal. Across the Suez Canal to the south lies Egypt. That's desert land. It's just as barren and sandy as it can be. Moving on up toward the middle of Israel, Jerusalem is located in approximately the mid point of that small nation. From

Jerusalem northward the topography changes rapidly. One sees fertile lands, crops that are abundant, water is in evidence, and everything is dramatically different in Upper Galilee from the Sinai.

In addition to those divisions or regions marked by topography, there were some regions marked out in Jesus' day along political lines. Herod the Great died in 4 B.C. At the time of his death, he divided Palestine among his sons. To Philip he gave Iturea and Trachonitis. He gave Galilee to Herod Antipas, and Archalaus got Judea and Samaria. When he divided this little land into regions, the populace erupted like a volcano. Archelaus soon, because of the political unrest and turmoil, was replaced by Quirinius. When we look in the second chapter of Luke, we find the same man referred to, but his name is spelled differently. His name is rendered Cyrenius. It was at the decree of Cyrenius that the taxation was made requiring the census. That census brought Mary and Joseph from Nazareth down to Bethlehem, the city of their childhood, to register.

During this period of time Palestine was just like a seething caldron. There was unrest, conflict, and turmoil on every hand, and it was all set off by the knowledge that Rome was going to universally tax the Jewish people. They rebelled against the idea of paying tribute to anyone save God alone.

It was at this time in history that the Zealot party came into great prominence, and it was then that they became clearly defined. They were fanatical in their patriotism. They were zealous for the law and were despisers of any foreign power. As they became coagulated in their opposition to Rome at this point in history, they began to attract to themselves an undesirable and unwanted element. These were adventurers and violent men. Soon that element within the Zealot party formed a hard core who came to be known as the "Sicarii" or the "Assassins." They got their name from that little dagger or sword called the *sica*. It was a slightly curved blade which could be concealed in the long flowing robes, in sleeves of the garments of that day, or perhaps tucked into the belt in an obscure fashion. It could be slipped out quickly and easily and plunged into the back of a Roman or a collaborator, and one could take flight before being apprehended. The *sica* was a lethal weapon. The Sicarii were the hard core of the Zealots who were murderous in their approach.

Things had gotten so bad in Palestine in Jesus' day that the Zealots turned against their own fellow countrymen. They were killing other Jews. They were suspicious of one another, and the Sicarii began to specialize in marking out for assassination certain Jews known to be collaborators with Rome. Any Jew who compromised with the Roman authorities, who entered into any treaty or agreement with Rome, was set apart for assassination. To pay taxes to the Romans was to betray God and country.

One of the most terrible times in all history was about A.D. 70 when the Roman General Titus, under orders of the Roman Senate, was dispatched to Jerusalem to quell the uprising. The uprising was led by the Zealots. They were trying once and for all to overthrow the yoke of bondage. Rome stood it as long as she could and finally decided that group of insubordinate, rebellious, cantankerous Jews were going to be quelled. Titus was given specific instructions to stop the conflict, to do whatever was necessary. One of the bloodiest chapters in human history centers in the war between the Jews and Romans in A.D. 70 in which the city of Jerusalem was obliterated from the face of the earth with hardly one stone left standing upon another.

When that transpired, not only were the Romans attacking from the outside but the Zealots, on the inside, were killing certain Jews. Jews who dared to suggest a compromise, those who were moderate in their approach, who saw the uselessness of the situation and suggested running up the white flag of surrender, were marked out to be murdered by the Sicarii. Finally, when it was apparent there was absolutely nothing that could be done, that the Romans by sheer weight of numbers and military power would be successful, about one thousand of the Zealots escaped Jerusalem. They made their way southward, down near the Dead Sea, to a world-famed spot called Masada.

Masada was built by Herod as a fortress. It was uniquely suited for the purpose. It was situated on a high hill with sheer cliffs. There was only one way of access to this fortress. When these nearly one thousand Zealots got to Masada, they destroyed the one avenue of entrance. When Titus finished his job at Jerusalem, he was determined to put down the last of the rebels, so he made his way to Masada. Upon arrival he saw the futility of trying to attack that fortress city, high on a hill with sheer cliffs surrounding it. He began a long, laborious task of building an earthen embankment from the ground all the way up the side, where chariots would be able to drive up, thus the equipment could be taken up with the soldiers and they could attack the fortress. It required almost two years to build the embankment. Finally it was finished and the first of the Roman soldiers went piling over the wall into Masada and they found almost a thousand Zealots dead. To a man they had taken their own lives rather than be captured by the invading Romans. This was the spirit that permeated this religious-political party. That was the spirit of the man Simon whom our Lord chose as one of his apostles.

Now observe the—

Conflict

—among the twelve. Does it seem strange to you that our Lord would choose two men among his twelve apostles who were mortal enemies? Matthew Levi, a Jew by birth, was a collaborator with Rome, having accepted Roman appointment to gather the taxes in behalf of the imperial government. Here is Simon the Zealot, a man who had sworn in blood to be a lifelong enemy of people like Matthew, yet living with him side by side with no hint of animosity or apparent intention to kill him. There's no indication in the New Testament that he ever tried to take the life of Matthew.

Simon the Zealot must have been the sort of man who had to nave a cause. He was waging constant warfare with someone some-where. He was always in conflict and was ready, at the snap of a finger, to lay down his life for his convictions. Why would such a man leave the Zealots, a cause which was accomplishing big things in guerilla warfare? Why would he, at the time of Jesus Christ, some forty years before the destruction of Jerusalem, leave the Zealot party to follow the nonbelligerent, unarmed, Galilean carpenter named Jesus? I'm sure only eternity can reveal the final answer to such a question, but the answer that satisfies me is that without doubt Simon saw in Jesus the sort of person, the sort of life, and the kind of kingdom that could produce lasting changes in humanity. He came to understand the truth of the words of Jesus that any kingdom that could be established by the sword can also be destroyed by the sword. Any kingdom set up on the basis of military might is subject to defeat by superior military might. But a kingdom set up on the permeating influence and power of love is a kingdom that can transcend all military barriers, and withstand the forces of military might. Undoubtedly Simon saw this in Jesus Christ. The power of God transformed this Simon and he found fulfillment in this life of discipleship.

We have revolutionaries today, some of whom claim identification with Jesus Christ. They say Jesus was a revolutionary. By all means he was, but he can in no way be identified with the revolutionaries of our time who take to the streets in armed rebellion, who destroy property, both public and private, and whose battle cry is "burn, baby, burn." Don't try to equate Jesus with that kind of revolutionary, for that ploy just won't work. Even those who have the sketchiest information about Jesus know that he never went about the establishment of his kingdom in any such way.

There are those who say that the way to change the world order is to burn. Others say the way to change the world order is to learn. They set out for an acquisition of knowledge. They seek all the education they possibly can get. Our institutions of higher learning are filled to overflowing, because "learn" has become a battle cry, and the way some people choose to revolutionize society. If that were the answer, would not our universities and college campuses be little havens of peace and tranquillity? Would not the faculty members be the ones who get along with the greatest love and brotherhood toward one another? If learning is the answer, why is it that faculty meeting rooms are places where civil wars are fought week in and week out? The absurdity of that approach is clearly apparent in our day.

Others say the answer to the problems and the revolution we must have is called earn, that the earning power of the average human being must be elevated to the point that there are no financial needs, no material deficiencies, where everyone has enough to buy everything he needs. That also includes most everything one might want! Earn.

You know, the revolution Jesus came into the world to perpetuate is called turn. Except we are converted, and that means to turn, and become like little children, we shall in no wise enter the kingdom of heaven. No, Jesus was not the kind of revolutionary we find up and down the streets, destroying property, crying out in a bloodthirsty fashion. Jesus was the kind of revolutionary whose change took place deep in the heart of a human being. It's the transforming power of God in a life filled with sin and iniquity.

One other word. Remember Simon's—

Consecration.

Among the twelve apostles we see the miracle of interpersonal relations. Let's face it. Under any other set of circumstances, Simon would have inserted his *sica* in Matthew's ribs and walked around him with it. Simon the Zealot, unlike so many of us, never tried to remake Jesus into his own mold. He didn't try to make a Zealot out of our Lord, rather he became a follower of Jesus Christ.

In your mind's eye, how do you picture our Lord? What's he going to be like when he comes again? Will he be an American? Will he be a Jew from Israel? Will he be white or black, brown or yellow? Will he be a Democrat or a Republican? Or will Jesus be a general to lead us in quelling the uprising of Red China, or maybe the USSR? Just what is Jesus going to be like in your thinking? It's pretty easy for us to fit Jesus into our mold, but it's a very difficult thing for us to fit our lives into his mold.

The name Simon appears in Acts 1:13, proving that he did not resign his commission after Calvary. He stayed faithful.

Maybe our generation will be smart enough someday to learn this lesson. The only experience that can erase our differences and make us truly brothers and sisters in Christ is the new birth. That's the only answer. Obviously both Simon and Matthew had that experience. It comes to any one of us when we follow the command of Jesus and turn from self, selfishness, and pride, and turn to him in humility and trust. When we come to the equation, inserting our name, Landrum Leavell equals nothing, we are there. When you start there, Christ has a foundation on which to build. As long as you try to come to Jesus, making him accept what you've done, pleading your cause, trying to tell him who you are, you have no foundation. It's sinking sand.

When you come to Jesus, not pleading your own cause, but stripped of all of your embellishments, standing in his presence equaling nothing, he's ready to take you. You can accept his invitation: "Come unto me, all ye that labour and are heavy laden, and I will give you rest. Take my yoke upon you, and learn of me." You can come just as you are. You don't have to get ready in some way before you come. When you come just like you are, you can find life in terms of its highest values. Only in Christ can you learn the tang, zest, and real challenge of life and discover the joy of consecration to a cause that is eternal.

If you're willing to turn from whatever it is that has deterred you and kept you from serving Christ and turn to him totally, saying, "In my hand no price I bring, Simply to Thy cross I cling," he'll take you just like that.

IX
JAMES—SON OF ALPHAEUS
Luke 6:15

I am personally grateful for an apostle like James, the son of Alphaeus. My gratitude stems from the total silence in the New Testament about this man. Someone quickly asks, "Do you mean you're grateful the New Testament doesn't tell us anything about him?" Really, I'd like to know more about James, the son of Alphaeus, but my gratitude stems from the fact that this man is almost completely overlooked, though he was one of the twelve apostles of our Lord. There's no mention made of him in the Bible. There's no word he ever spoke recorded, no deed he ever did described. His name is not to be found in the headlines of the New Testament journal, but thank God his name is found in the Lamb's book of life. That's the important thing.

He's one of three men named James found in the New Testament. Unfortunately, he is woefully dwarfed by the other two by this name. One of these, of course, was James the apostle, the son of Zebedee. He was one of the inner circle composed of Peter, James, and John. They were with our Lord on a number of significant occasions and seemed to be the closest friends our Lord had on this earth. The New Testament writers give him a significant place in their records.

The second man bearing the name James is described as the brother of our Lord. Though he was not an apostle, he was a recognized leader in the church in Jerusalem following the resurrection from the dead of his half brother, the Lord Jesus Christ.

In the fourth century A.D., a Latin scholar named Jerome translated the Scriptures from the original language into the Latin. Also called Hieronymus, he is noted today for his translation of the Latin Vulgate. He has been afforded sainthood by the Roman Catholic Church. Jerome worked for a time for the Pope in Rome, but upon the death of the Pope he came back to the Holy Land, settled in Bethlehem, and there spent the remainder of his life in a scholastic setting.

Travelers to Bethlehem today go through the Church of the Nativity. Just to the side of the Church of the Nativity is an open courtyard, in the center of which is a statue. That statue is in memory of Jerome. It was in or very near that spot that he spent the last years of his life studying, translating, and interpreting.

Naturally those who give veneration to and worship the virgin Mary try to make some explanation about the obvious biblical account that she had other children than our Lord. The theory of perpetual virginity granted to Mary by papal decree does not leave room for Mary and Joseph to have had other children. Jerome, translating the Bible from the original languages into the Latin, solved that problem with a very simple device. His method of eliminating the problem was to change the word "brother" to the word "cousin," so in his translation, Mary had no children save Jesus. These others listed in the original account as brothers become "cousins." Now there is absolutely no scriptural or linguistic authority for such an interpretation, but it removes a major barrier for those who worship the virgin Mary.

Look again with me at James, the son of Alphaeus. I want you to recall his—

Insignificance.

We find an interesting insight in Mark 2:14. "And as he," that is Jesus, "passed by, he saw Levi." This is the other name for Matthew, one of the apostles. "He saw [Matthew] Levi, the son of Alphaeus sitting at the receipt of custom." You'll notice in our text, Luke 6:15, we are told that James, the apostle whom we are studying, was a son of Alphaeus.

Now look at one other verse. In Mark 15, beginning in verse 40, we have the account of the crucifixion of our Lord and the people who were standing around watching his death. There were also women looking on from afar off, among whom were Mary Magdalene, and Mary, the mother of James the Less and of Joses. Two of her boys are named. James the Less was the son of Alphaeus, he was a son of Mary, and he also had a brother named Joses.

When we merge these accounts we learn a great deal about a man named Alphaeus. If Alphaeus is one and the same man, he was the father of Matthew, who became an apostle; the father of James, who became an apostle; the father of a son named Joses, who apparently was also a follower of our Lord. And Alphaeus' wife was present at the crucifixion.

When you further merge these accounts, you'll find that this family had some problems. Think of their lives before Christ, B.C. They had a boy who was a black sheep. He was so money mad, so in love with cash, that he was willing to get cash by selling out his country and becoming a collaborator with Rome. Everybody looked with disdain upon a publican, which Matthew was.

They had another son named James, called James the Less, or James the son of Alphaeus, who in the record of the twelve apostles is always associated with Simon Zelotes, or the Zealot. So here was one of their other sons associated with the fanatical right-wing movement, the Zealot movement, which resorted to mayhem and murder to accomplish their goals. Being associated idealogically with Simon the Zealot put him at outs with his brother Matthew.

Then Alphaeus and his wife Mary had at least one other child, a son named Joses, who must have been a middle-of-the-road sort of person. He probably did not agree with his brother Matthew nor with his brother James but took a little more conservative approach to life. His life-style may have been in between the other two.

Now friend, if you think you have family problems, how would you have felt if you were Alphaeus and Mary? They had two sons who adopted life-styles that were radically different. One, living for the coin of the realm, had sold his soul to Rome. The other son was associated with the Zealot party, trying to eliminate by assassination all of the collaborators with Rome! That's as far removed as two sons could possibly be.

Think of their lives before Christ and after Christ. What is it that could come in and take a fragmented family like that, coagulate it, bring it together in a unity of purpose and oneness of spirit, and make that family what it ought to be in love, mutual admiration, and respect? There's no power on earth which could perform that miracle except the power of Jesus Christ. When Christ came in with that great unifying experience we call the new birth, he made brothers who despised each other love one another and give themselves to a common cause. Alphaeus and Mary had two sons in the ministry and another boy who followed Jesus. What a tribute to a godly family brought together in Christ.

The Gospel writers tell us that Peter and Andrew were brothers. They tell us James and John were brothers, but they don't tell us that Matthew and James were brothers. Does this mean they were not, and that Alphaeus was not one but two different men? Not necessarily. This can rather point to the insignificance of James the Less.

What a demeaning designation that is. Some scholars say it refers to his stature, that he was a small man physically, therefore they nicknamed him that. That nickname would be roughly equivalent to "Little Jim" today, James the Less. It's also possible that the name James the Less was a separating designation, marking him as apart from James the son of Zebedee, or from James the brother of our Lord. No one can say for sure, and there's no way we'll ever know this side of eternity. The fact is James the son of Alphaeus, or James the Less, is a forgotten disciple.

I imagine that this is the first material many have read on this man. Even the legends and traditions that grew up about him are limited. Legend holds that he preached in Persia and died the death of a martyr by crucifixion, but even this has no positive substantiation. Now we'll talk about the—

Investment

—of this insignificant man. James the Less was eclipsed not only by the other Jameses but also by his brother Matthew. The fact of greatest comfort to me is that Jesus needed this man and chose him to be an apostle. When the apostles were called out, it wasn't on a voluntary basis. I believe there are many tasks in the kingdom for which we can accept volunteers, but I'm convinced there are some tasks in the kingdom of God for which persons must be hand-picked.

I believe this is true in the call to the ministry. God handpicks men to preach the gospel. I believe it's also true in certain places in the work of a church, for sometimes very unfortunate volunteers come forward to assume responsible places. When Jesus wanted men into whose care and keeping he would entrust the propagation of the gospel, he didn't extend his arms and ask: "Who will volunteer? Who would like to serve in this capacity?" Jesus went to these men one by one, called them, and trained them. Jesus needed James the Less. He called him and he commissioned him. When he did, that opened vast new horizons of service for this man who had been so insignificant.

It's obvious to all who have studied the New Testament that James the Less was faithful to his calling, for his name appears in the list of the twelve found in the book of Acts. That proves that after the resurrection, James remained true as a Christian witness for the Lord Jesus Christ.

Can we not assume that this James represents the quiet, the silent majority, the forgotten, or the little people in life? Can we not personally identify with this man James? Most of us will never have our names in headlines. We'll never get wide publicity. We won't be known from coast to coast or even throughout the county in which we live. The tremendous truth is that Jesus Christ needs that kind of person and has a work for every Christian to perform! That work may not afford you popularity or publicity, but it will afford you, like James, an opportunity to be faithful. If you are, that's what counts.

I am reminded of one of the teachings of our Lord that sounds strange to our ears. That teaching is that the judgments of the world cannot be equated with the judgment of God. Jesus said the first shall be last and the last shall be first (Mark 10:31). In that statement he was reminding us that though we may have the acclaim, the confidence of all humanity, though we may be first in the minds of other people on this earth, that does not guarantee us a place of prominence in the kingdom of God. God doesn't judge humans on the same basis on which we judge one another! God will not mete out rewards in eternity on the basis of human evaluations! God is going to judge motive, and that's something not known by other humans. You can't know the motive of someone else. You may suspect it; you may think you do; you may say, "Oh, I know why he's doing that," or, "I know what made her do what she did." Friend, that's just a suspicion. You don't know, but God does. It's for that reason that Jesus said the first, that is those who may think they're first or those to whom the world affords a place of priority, are going to be last and those who may be considered by the world to be last are going to be first.

There was an obscure dry goods clerk in the 1850's in London, England. His name was George Williams. He was a quiet, forgotten little man. He never became prime minister. He never sat in Parliament. He never made headlines and never wrote a book. He didn't lead any armies in battle, nor did he ever have anyone make a fuss over him. All that he ever did was to invite some of his Christian friends to join him in prayer and Christian fellowship during their free hours. As a result of that very inauspicious beginning, today we have a worldwide organization known as the YMCA.

There's no way for us to know how many people James the son of Alphaeus influenced for good as a follower of Jesus Christ. But eternity is going to reveal the good done by people who were less than prominent.

Let me conclude by pointing to several—

Implications

—I find in the life and ministry of James. The first is, there are no nobodies in God's plan. Did you get me? Do you believe it? You don't believe it if you erroneously say: "What I do doesn't matter. I'm only hurting myself, not anyone else." Maybe the fallacy of which you are guilty is: "Well, I won't be missed. No one will know whether I'm there or not." Or maybe your fallacy is: "My contribution doesn't mean much. It's so small it just doesn't matter." Listen to me, friend, that's the devil's attack. That's not God's way, for God has a place for every person he saves! He has a purpose for every life he touches. I don't care how insignificant you are. I don't care whether or not the only recognition you have is that your name is included on the roll of a church membership file. You're somebody to God and he has something he wants you to do.

You may say: "I'm like James. Nothing I ever said or did was important enough to be written down." My friend, that doesn't matter. Jesus knew James, loved James, and called James. Thank God, James was faithful to his calling.

It's hardly possible any of us will be like Simon Peter and preach a sermon comparable to the one at Pentecost, but that's not important. We can be found faithful. We can render our service inconspicuously for Jesus Christ and his kingdom. There are no nobodies in God's plan. He has a place for you and he's aware of where you are. When you move from one community to another, you're not taking God by surprise, you're not hiding from him, you're not in a spot where he doesn't know your address. Wherever you are, if you belong to him, he's got a place for you and a job for you. You have a responsibility for finding that job and performing it for his honor and glory.

Not many of us will ever achieve the fame of Billy Graham, Oral

Roberts, Bob Harrington, or a lot of the others. That's not important. God didn't make but one Billy Graham, and if he'd wanted some more, he would have made them! He wants me to fill the place that he has for me, and he wants you to fill the place he has for you! No one is overlooked. No one is left out. God loved you enough to save you, and he has enough confidence in you to afford you a place of service.

The second implication—the Jameses outnumber the Simon Peters in every generation. There are a lot more Christians in the category of James, the son of Alphaeus, than there are in the category of Simon Peter. Where one gains personal recognition and fame, hundreds will go unnoticed and unrecognized.

It may be the obscure teacher who is working with younger children in a Sunday School class, working faithfully week after week. Oftentimes that unnoticed and unsung teacher is dealing with children who are restless or disinterested or who have emotional problems coming from broken homes and a sense of insecurity, but that teacher works on for the glory of God and the honor of Jesus.

Let me tell you something. If your motive is right, you're not ever going to resign, saying, "Nobody appreciates me." Friend, the only one who is supposed to appreciate you is Jesus, and nothing you do is unnoticed by him. He has a record of your service. He knows your every word and deed. He has a tabulation on you, and he's the one who is going to do the rewarding! You don't have to worry about what people think, for if you're serving to honor Christ and to live a life of fidelity to him, there's no reason ever for you to resign! You can keep on serving, keep on experiencing the sense of satisfaction that comes through faithfulness, even if you have no other satisfaction in life.

There are far more Jameses than there are Simon Peters. Statistics don't tell the whole story. Maybe your class is small. Maybe you don't have a large number, but who knows, out of that class there may come a Billy Graham, or a Florence Nightingale, or an R. G. LeTourneau, or a W. A. Criswell. Who knows? You fill the place

God has for you and your name will be listed on his books according to his evaluation of your service.

Of the 3000 people saved on the day of Pentecost, all we have is a record of the name of the preacher. Acts doesn't say anything about all those who were out personally witnessing and sharing their faith which brought about the 3000 conversions. But I can guarantee that every one of those 120 witnesses who went out from that prayer meeting under the impulse of the possession of the Holy Spirit witnessed fervently to their faith. Simon Peter is the one to whom we give credit for the results at Pentecost, but I think God's going to give the credit to the people who did the sharing. All Simon did was stand and proclaim the gospel and give the invitation. Somebody else had done the eyeball-to-eyeball, personal soul-winning and the sharing of his faith.

One other implication here. It's implied with James, and all the way through the New Testament, that Jesus Christ is the divine multiplier. Just as he took the loaves and fishes of a lad and multiplied them to feed a vast multitude, so Jesus Christ can take the meager loaves and fishes of your life and mine and multiply these for his own glory. You see, we don't have to give Jesus a lot. All we have to give him is what we have, and what we have to offer him may not be equivalent to what someone else offers him. Yet if we give him all we have, like that obscure, insignificant, little boy who surrendered his lunch, Jesus can take it and can use it with the greatest effectiveness in the kingdom.

Someone once asked Dwight L. Moody, "What makes you think that you've got a monopoly on the Holy Spirit?" His answer was, "I don't have a monopoly on him, he has a monopoly on me." Dear friend, that's the secret of greatness. The secret of greatness does not revolve around superior talent, or ability to articulate the faith, or the amount of spare time that you might be able to invest in service for Christ. The secret of greatness is your surrender of what you have, not by comparison with someone else, but on the basis of what Christ has given you. That's all he holds you responsible for. He doesn't hold you responsible for anyone else, just for yourself. If you, like James, the son of Alphaeus, give him what you have, surrender it to him totally, he'll take it and use it, and when life is over and you stand before him in judgment he'll reward you for your motive and faithfulness.

Maybe you live in a community and don't have a local church home. Friend, it doesn't matter whether you are going to be there two weeks, two months, or two years. What does matter is how you are going to spend those weeks, months, or years. Are you going to spend them for Christ in an open, unashamed witness for him? Are you going to seclude yourself and become a recluse and not let anybody know whether or not you are a Christian? That's the sort of thing God is going to hold you responsible for. It's not how long you live, but how you live. It's not the quantity of life, it's the quality of life God's going to evaluate. Methuselah lived 969 years, but that's all we know. We don't know how he lived any one of those years. He lived longer than any man has ever lived, but the Bible doesn't tell us a thing about how he spent that time. What have you accomplished if you can live to 95 or 100 years of age? That's not important. How do you spend the years you have?

Jesus didn't live but about thirty-three years, but quality was the important thing about his life. That's the important thing with us, too.

X
PHILIP
John 1:43-44

Frequently in the New Testament we discover more than one person with the same name. The writers seemed to assume that for their readers there was little chance of confusion. For instance, three different men with the name James are mentioned prominently in the New Testament.

There are two different men in the New Testament named Philip. The man whom we study now is the apostle. The second man in the New Testament named Philip is a deacon. He's first mentioned in the book of Acts as being one of the those seven men of good report who were called out from among the membership of the church to be servants of the church. Deacons are servants, and this second Philip was a deacon. We learn more from the New Testament about him than about the apostle.

Through the book of Acts everywhere deacon Philip went this God-fearing, soul-winning Christian left a trail of converts behind him. In Acts 8 it was deacon Philip who led in a great layman's revival in Samaria. This would be roughly comparable to one of us going in a revival effort to Red China, Cuba, Russia, or any nation we ordinarily consider our antagonist. Deacon Philip went to the Samaritans without any view to their race or the animosity which existed between Jews and Samaritans, and he preached the gospel of Jesus Christ.

So great was that in-depth revival, led by a layman, that perhaps the most infamous and best known individual in the community was saved. He was a sorcerer, or a magician, and the genuineness of his conversion experience is proven in that he attached himself to Philip, went everywhere he went, and tried to learn everything he could about the gospel. He was present when some of the apostles came down from Jerusalem, laid hands upon the Samaritans, and they received the Holy Spirit. Simon the sorcerer wanted to know by what power they did that and offered them money in order to receive that power for himself. Peter pronounced a curse upon him for desiring to buy a spiritual gift. Then Peter urged him to repent, that this sorcerer might be changed from his greed and lust for the things that money could buy and for self-advancement.

Deacon Philip not only witnessed to the Samaritans, who were considered enemies of the Jews, but he sat down in a chariot and won a "soul brother" to Christ, a black man, an Ethiopian eunuch. Philip, the deacon, caught a vision of world conquest in the name of Christ. He understood there were no barriers nor limitations to those with whom he might share his faith. Everyone he saw was a possible recipient of the love of God, and he shared that love which he had come to know in Christ.

Deacon Philip was the host of the apostle Paul when he visited his home town of Caesarea. Acts 21 tells us that the deacon had four daughters who also had the gift of prophecy. What an outstanding person he was!

The man whom we now study was, in his own right, equally outstanding. I'd like to point you to some of the—

Influences

—brought to bear upon the life of the apostle Philip. Most notable among them surely was his hometown. The text tells us that he was raised in Bethsaida. You'll recall that little village mentioned many times in the New Testament. It was the home of Peter and Andrew, who were also apostles. It's probable that it was also the home of James and John.

The name Bethsaida means "fish house." The village was located on the Sea of Galilee where these fishermen earned their livelihood. It was situated on the far northern coast, adjacent to the city of Capernaum and at the mouth of the Jordan River. The Jordan flows down into the Sea of Galilee and then out of the Sea of Galilee southward to eventually form the Dead Sea, from which there is no outlet. Living in that place and having contact with these other men surely was a tremendous influence upon his life.

These other fishermen were devout Jews. They entertained the hope of the coming of the Messiah. They were anticipating the arrival of the holy One of Israel, and that blessed hope must have rubbed off on the lives of others in their circle of acquaintances.

Not only were they devout Jews, but these fishermen attached themselves to the greatest evangelist of that century prior to Christ. They followed John the Baptist and learned a great deal from him. Everywhere John held a revival crusade, these fishermen would attend the meetings. They were supporters of John the Baptist. They must have encouraged him. In all likelihood, they gave some financial backing for his ministry. Without a doubt they patted him on the back and congratulated him upon the forthright messages he preached, straight from the heart of God to the hearts of the people. They must have been in the crowd saying, "amen," or at least the Greek equivalent to "amen" in the first century.

Bethsaida was a busy, thriving community. It was the province capital of Iturea. The respected tetrarch was named Philip. This province capital was much like our present day county seat towns. It was the seat of local government and enjoyed a building boom. For ten years Bethsaida was a growing community. As public officials, soldiers, traders, and builders came there, the economy constantly expanded. Possibly it was like my own wonderful city of Wichita Falls, Texas.

In recent months new industries have announced their intention to locate here. There is a building boom. Construction permits are going up and up. Bank deposits are up. Everything in our community economically is healthy. We can be grateful for that. This same thing was characteristic of Bethsaida under the administration of Philip the tetrarch and it's probable that this apostle, a Jew, got his Greek name from the tetrarch. His parents likely had admiration for this man who administered justice fairly and who led their community and area in such a fine way. It's probable that they gave his name to their son.

Another influence on the life of Philip the apostle was that of his friends. Growing up in the community with Andrew, Peter, James, John, and other God-fearing Jews, he must have had a background of religion and religious fervor. Those who were committed to the things of the Jewish religion were men who believed what they said they believed and gave themselves wholly to it.

But the greatest influence on the life of Philip came through his contact with Jesus Christ. The call of Christ to Philip received only one sentence in the New Testament. Jesus found Philip and said, "Follow me." Just a brief statement of call, but what a tremendous influence it was on his life. The call came in the divine sequence. Jesus found Philip. This same procedure has occurred untold millions of times through all generations. This is God's way.

It has been well said that religion is man's search for God. The Christian faith, by contrast, is God's search for man. God took the initiative. The Christian faith reveals a loving God, who in the Garden of Eden took the initiative to seek man after he had willfully rebelled. Adam and Eve didn't look for God; God came looking for them. They were the ones who had sinned, but in his love and desire to offer forgiveness, God sought them out. All through the pages of the Bible we find the divine initiative being in that sequence: God seeking man.

In the New Testament Jesus Christ came as the culmination of God's revelation. Again it was God who came to man in human form. He chose to live among men, and it was God who offered himself for the sins of man in the person of Jesus Christ. What a tremendous influence Jesus had upon the life of Philip.

Jesus described in parabolic form the divine initiative. He told us the parable of a wayward sheep and indicated man is like that wayward sheep. Jesus said man is like a lost coin. A lost coin is out of circulation. It's absolutely no good. It's worth nothing so far as its intended purpose is concerned. Man is like that in his lost condition. Jesus said man is like a rebellious teenager, a prodigal boy who dares to look into the face of his father who loves him more than any other person on the face of the earth and say, "I'm leaving home."

After describing man as a wayward sheep and a lost coin and a prodigal son, Jesus told us what God is like. He said God is like a shepherd, out on a dark, lonely hillside, maybe on a windy, stormy night, looking for that wayward sheep, risking his life in the darkness for the one hundredth sheep. Jesus said God is like that concerned housewife who literally turned her household upside down, who swept out every nook and cranny in the house until she found the coin that was lost. God is like that housewife. That's the divine initiative. This is the divine sequence.

Jesus said God is like that father. He'd given up his son for lost, but one day looking down the road he saw his son heading home. He rushed down that road with tears streaming down his cheeks and with open arms welcomed that boy back into the home which he had rejected and from which he had turned in rebellion. The influence of Jesus Christ on the life of Philip was the influence of a loving God who seeks mankind in its lost condition. That influence never diminished, for Philip became engaged in the divine activity as a laborer together with God, sharing what he knew to be true about Jesus Christ.

One preacher, preaching to preachers, stated there are two things we preachers must never do. A preacher must never leave Jesus on the cross. He's got to get Jesus down off the cross, into the tomb, and then back from the dead on the third day, alive forevermore. What a terrible injustice we do people if we simply picture Jesus as the crucified Savior. He is the living Christ.

Did you catch the phrase in Romans 10:9? That verse states, "That if thou shalt confess with thy mouth the Lord Jesus, and shalt believe in thine heart that God hath raised him from the dead, thou shalt be saved." Listen to me, friend, if you don't believe that Jesus is the living Christ, you're not saved. A very vital part of your salvation comes in the knowledge that Christ, who was crucified, buried, and who rose from the grave, is alive forevermore. Until you come to know this living Christ in a personal encounter, you have not experienced salvation. Not only does Christ come into your heart in the moment of conversion, Christ lives in your heart every day of your life and he lives out his life in you in proportion to your surrender.

That preacher said the other thing preachers must never do is leave the prodigal son in the far country. He's got to get the boy home. When the lost boy takes the first step in turning around, he finds God has already come to the far country to meet him. He has run down the road with open arms, with tears of joy to welcome him back into the family he rejected.

The validity of Philip's experience with Jesus Christ is proven in the customary activity of a Christian. Philip began to look for others who needed to be saved. Isn't that the proof of the pudding? When you have something that's so real you must share it with someone else, that's the acid test. If it's not real to you, then there's no compulsion to share it. If Christ is not alive in your heart, you're not apt to want to tell someone else about him.

These are some of the influences brought upon Philip's life. Now, I want us to think for a moment of his—

Intellect.

From the brief scriptural information we have, it's apparent that Philip was a practical man. We could call him a thinking man's apostle.

The four incidents in which Philip appears in the New Testament are all recorded in John's Gospel. There's the time of his call, the feeding of the five thousand, the Last Supper, and his encounter with the inquiring Greeks who came seeking Jesus.

In the miracle of feeding the multitude, surely it was to strengthen the faith of Philip and the other apostles that caused Jesus to ask how these people could be fed. The answer of Philip was that "two hundred pennyworth" would not be enough to feed such a vast throng. Philip was thinking only in terms of the money Judas carried for the apostles in the bag. He wasn't thinking in terms of the power of God in Jesus Christ. He was a practical man, and he had figured out how much money it would take to feed each individual. He knew the stores nearby didn't have that much bread. He was merely describing an impossible task. He had the ability to survey the crowd, and with a mind that worked like a calculator or a computer, he was able to come up with how much money it would take. He had a sharp mind.

In his encounter with Nathanael, it would have been easy for Philip to wander off in a meaningless theological argument, but his response to Nathanael was that of a practical businessman whose mind operated in that way. Rather than argue with him about the "product" he was trying to sell, he simply said, "Come and see." He didn't have to answer a lot of questions. He didn't have to have memorized answers. All he had to do was to bring Nathanael to Jesus.

Have you ever desperately wanted to ask a question but failed to do so for fear you might be thought stupid? Thank God, the apostles asked some of those stupid questions because they received answers that have been blessing Christians through all the centuries.

Thomas asked such a question. In John 14, Thomas simply could not contain himself. He asked Jesus how the apostles could possibly know the way, since they didn't have any idea where Jesus was going. Jesus said, "I am the way, the truth, and the life: no man cometh unto the Father, but by me." In that same chapter it was Philip who said, "Show us the Father, and it sufficeth us." Jesus said no man could come to the Father but by him. Philip wanted to know how he could know the Father. Jesus answered with the basic theological axiom of the Christian faith, "He that hath seen me hath seen the Father." That's the sum and substance of it all. It's pointed out in place after place in the New Testament. The basic affirmation of the Christian faith is, "God was in Christ, reconciling the world unto himself." That is either true or false. If it's true, it's the most spectacular thought that ever dawned upon the consciousness of man. If it's false, Jesus Christ is the world's foremost liar. "He that hath seen me hath seen the Father."

Do you ever wonder what God is like? Do you ever try to describe God in your own words? Do you somehow think that God is a capricious parent sitting on a throne far removed from this earth, picking out people like you and saying, "Ah-ha, I'm going to get him." Do you think that when a loved one dies, God has picked you out for a little extra punishment? Do you think that when your health is gone or your fortune has been lost, this is God's way of getting even with you?

Listen to me, friend! If you want to know what God is like, look at Jesus! What did Jesus do when people died? He never encountered a funeral procession that he didn't break it up. He called the dead back to life and sent the mourners home rejoicing. How did Jesus react in the presence of sickness? He healed every sick person he ever saw. Do you think he wants you to be sick? Do you think he sends afflictions upon you to punish you? "He that hath seen me," Jesus said, "hath seen the Father." If you are one of those for whom seeing is believing, look at Jesus and you'll find out what kind of God he represents, for he is God.

He came to reveal to us that God loves us and that God takes the divine initiative in trying to bring us back to himself. Because he was unashamed to ask, Philip got an answer that has blessed every Christian from that day till this.

I have one other word. That's the word—

Involvement.

That Philip was a missionary goes without saying. He didn't require a census or prospect card, a visitation supper, or the motivation of a pastor or some friend to get him out witnessing to lost people. He turned to the first person he met and shared Christ, and that person was Nathanael. Even if he had known how Nathanael might react, Philip did not hesitate.

In his involvement in sharing his faith he didn't argue with anybody. He just pointed them to Jesus. When the Greeks came to Jerusalem they looked up Philip, possibly because his name was of Greek origin. Here again, not wishing to debate or argue he just took them to Jesus. He knew that the presence of Jesus would outweigh whatever a disciple might say.

Every time we see Philip in the Gospels, he's involved in great themes. He's involved in sharing Christ, and that's the greatest theme of Christian living. He was involved in breaking bread and feeding hungry multitudes. He was involved in grasping the meaning of the cross. He was involved in the question-and-answer period in seeking to determine how we as human beings can know God. The keen mind of this practical man was clouded as he tried to grasp the meaning of God, the God who made this universe and the world and all that's in it, who put every star in all the infinities of space. How can one mind grasp that kind of God? So he asked a question. Jesus invited him to look at him if he wanted to know what God is like, for he and the Father are one. "He that hath seen me hath seen the Father."

A very wealthy patient was suffering a wide variety of aches and pains. He went to doctor after doctor, yet his maladies continued. Finally he consulted a very able physician who made this prescription. He told the rich man, "Go to work. Live on five dollars a day and earn that five dollars by hard labor." What an unusual prescription, but it was valid!

Maybe you're suffering from spiritual apathy and don't know why. Maybe your Christian faith has lost its vitality, its zest, its tang. Maybe you've got a dark brown taste in your mouth about the whole business. Friend, if you are suffering from the spiritual "blahs," I have a prescription for you. Get to work. Like Philip the apostle, get to work bringing people to Jesus, and I can guarantee you the cure for every spiritual malady you have. If you get busy, involved in the things that Jesus was involved in, you'll find a new tang and zest in life and in your relationship to our Lord. Not only will your own spiritual problems be solved, but you'll be able to make an eternal contribution to the lives of other people.

XI
JUDAS—SON OF JAMES
Luke 6:16

Because the New Testament tells us that there were twelve apostles, we must make the effort to harmonize the various lists of the twelve men. In the Gospels and Acts their names appear differently. In comparing these lists it may seem that there are thirteen, fourteen, or even fifteen different men named as apostles.

The man whom we study now is the most difficult to identify of any of the twelve. Jerome, a fourth-century church historian and scholar, called this man "Trinomius." That word means "man with three names." In Matthew 10:3 he is referred to as "Lebbaeus, whose surname was Thaddaeus." There are two different names. In our text he is referred to as Judas, the brother of James. In John 14:22 he is referred to as Judas, not Iscariot. That's the fourth designation. In Acts 13, following Luke 6:16, the reading is Judas, the brother of James. Since Luke is the author of both the Gospel and Acts, it stands to reason that he would use the same designation in both places. Four different references are given in the five accounts of this man.

Your immediate question is where do you get the subject, "Judas, Son of James"? The only reference found in the King James Version is to Judas, brother of James. But later translations all change this to "son of" rather than "brother of." If your translation is King James, you'll notice that the two words "the brother" are in italics. Universally in the King James Version italicized words are not in the original manuscripts but are inserted for the purpose of clarification. The Greek has only "Judas of James," and the King James translators felt it should be interpreted as "brother of" rather than "son of."

In case after case in the New Testament, individuals are identified with their fathers. It's rare to find a man identified with his brother. In our earlier study of the apostles we gave consideration to Simon Bar-jona, "son of Jona." The identification in most cases is with a man's father and not a brother. The weight of evidence is in favor of making this identification Judas, the son of James, rather than Judas, the brother of James.

The name Thaddaeus means "courageous one" or "the bold." The name Lebbaeus means "hearty" or "the hearty one." Since these names are given this man whom we identify as Judas, the son of James, we can decide with some degree of certainty that these names were descriptive of his character. That being true, we can say this apostle was a friendly, affable extrovert, the kind of man who easily made new friends, an outgoing individual who spoke to everyone he met. Undoubtedly, he would have made an outstanding salesman or perhaps an expert in the field of personnel management.

Let's look a little more closely at his life and his witness. I'd like for us to look at his—

Response

—to the teachings of Jesus. This can be discerned from the only sentence found in the New Testament recording words from his lips. In John's Gospel Judas asked Jesus how he could manifest himself to his apostles and his followers without showing himself to all people. We must take the context in which this question was asked in order to understand it. It's found in John 14. That's the beloved chapter which our Lord began by saying, "Let not your hearts be troubled: ye believe in God, believe also in me." In that passage Jesus stated he would be leaving them, "I go to prepare a place for you." Though he predicted his departure he also promised his presence, his comfort, and a revelation of himself. It's in that context that Judas, the son of James asked his question.

At least one later manuscript, written after the New Testament, identifies this man as Judas the Zealot. If that be accurate, he was one of the super-patriots of the first century. He was one of those individuals who never accepted the dominance of Rome and lived for the day when that yoke of bondage could be overthrown. Though Rome far outnumbered these people in military might, in soldiers, armament, chariots, horses, and everything else, there still burned in the hearts of these patriots a desire to cast off that bondage and become free men. The Zealots were not only striving for freedom, they wanted recognition and world power.

Jesus had spoken to the apostles about his leaving, and this patriot who had never given up his hope for freedom was inspired to ask Jesus something connected with his departure that would have to do with the future after he was gone. Against the background of these incomparable promises in John 14, Judas wanted to know how Jesus could manifest himself to his people without revealing himself to everyone. How could Jesus give peace and freedom while they were still under the yoke of Rome? Judas was confused. He was absolutely certain that Rome would have to be defeated, and if Rome were defeated, the mistress of the world, everybody would know it. Judas couldn't put all these facts together.

Keep in mind that a few weeks prior to this Jesus came into the city of Jerusalem riding a lowly donkey at the time of his triumphal entry. When he entered the city of Jerusalem in that fashion he manifested himself to his followers as the Lord of all and the King of glory. Everyone in Jerusalem knew it. They lined the streets. They shouted his name and cried their hosannas of praise to God. They strewed the streets with palm branches on that Palm Sunday. Some even placed their coats out on the street over which the donkey could walk as Jesus entered Jerusalem. How can someone manifest himself to his followers without everybody knowing it?

Jesus had told his disciples he was the Son of God, the Lord of glory, but that was revealed to everyone in Jerusalem. Judas just could not understand. Judas Thaddaeus Lebbaeus had in mind the same sort of thing that happened in Jerusalem on the day of the triumphal entry, everyone knowing what was going on, and everyone joining in the great celebration.

Now Jesus is talking about leaving them without capitalizing on that glorious opportunity. Judas wanted to know what was taking place. When he asked our Lord this question, Jesus gave a—

Reply.

We can be grateful for Judas' dilemma, and we can thank God that he voiced his question. Jesus replied it was impossible for him to reveal himself to anyone other than those who loved him and obeyed his commands. That's about as pointed and direct as you can make it, isn't it? It's a fact that needs to be emphasized today.

Maybe the reason for your spiritual stagnation, your spiritual illiteracy, is that you have not obeyed Jesus. There's not a Christian anywhere but who knows to do much more than he has done in kingdom citizenship. The reason we are spiritually impotent when we ought to be dynamos of power for God is disobedience! Jesus said in John 14:23, "If a man love me, he will keep my words: and my Father will love him, and we will come unto him, and make our abode with him." Jesus Christ abides in the human heart when one is obedient.

The New Testament tells us it's possible for human beings to grieve the Holy Spirit. How can you grieve him? You grieve him when you disappoint him by disobedience. When you know what a child of God should do in a given situation and you refuse to do it, you have grieved the Holy Spirit. When you obey him, you exalt him. Maybe the reason that so many of us are spiritual pygmies when we ought to be spiritual giants is our willful disobedience of God's known will!

On the other hand, this is the reason Christians can be so confident of the will of God while the world is totally ignorant of God's will. I know a lot of people who have gotten up tight over the situation in the Middle East. Even some theologians have chosen to refer to the Middle East problems as the dress rehearsal for Armageddon. That may well be. It's not surprising to me, however, for we were never told that we would enjoy peace in this world between nations or between men. We were told that wars would continue. We are told that in the last days things are going to grow worse and worse, and that men would be deceivers and liars. That includes men in prominent places. We've been told in the Word of God that men would turn from their natural function and would become perverted, with men loving men and women loving women. I'm not surprised at this. You see, Christians know the will of God and we know that our Lord has told us that these things will occur. All of this is to take place prior to the second coming of Christ and it doesn't cause us undue anxiety, except as we look forward to the return of Jesus Christ in power. So our Lord is simply reiterating in John 14:23 what he said in John 14:15, "If ye love me, keep my commandments." That's the test.

I'm fed up with the mouthing of pious platitudes and the smooth shibboleths which many have learned to repeat regarding "love." Some folk think all that's required of Christians is that we just "love." I want to tell you that's a half gospel, and a half gospel is no gospel! The love of God is conditioned by law. God's laws are as valid today as they were in the day in which they were spoken.

I heard a local preacher on radio not long ago pointing out very meticulously why Christians are no longer obligated to the Ten Commandments. That's hogwash! That's pure poppycock! Don't tell me that "love" is all that's expected of a Christian, for Jesus said, "If you love me, [obey] me!" That's as plain as the nose on your face, and if you obey him, you'll know his will. You won't be wandering around wondering which way is up. You'll have an idea about what's going on in the world and in your own life. God reveals his will to those who obey him. It's not enough to say, "Oh, I 'love' everybody. I've found the love of God in Jesus." That's great, friend, you've taken one step when you do that. Then you find out that

that love is governed by certain requirements. You're expected to do some things in response if that love is real and genuine.

What is the Spirit-filled life? You find a lot of people going off the deep end on that subject, and the tragedy is that they are doing it under the guise of a do-nothing Christianity. If you're Spirit-filled, where are your fruits? That's the big question. Your fruit is not to sit around in a little clandestine group and speak in an unknown tongue or simply to pore over the Word of God. That's not immoral, but it is never to be an end in itself. If it becomes an end, that's proof you're not filled with the Holy Spirit, for the Holy Spirit impels to service. He won't let you be content to sit around and merely study the Book. He doesn't allow you to be at peace after meeting in a small group and speaking in an unknown tongue. When the Holy Spirit is in control, you'll be out sharing Jesus, for fruitfulness is one of the characteristics of discipleship. What is the fruit of a Christian? Another Christian. Just like the fruit of a pecan tree is pecans, the fruit of an apple tree is apples, the fruit of a Christian is another Christian.

The power of the Holy Spirit is the power of Jesus Christ, and if you say you've got the Holy Spirit, that's the same as saying you've got Jesus. If you have him you'll exalt him and not any other.

In verse 26 of John 14 Jesus told Judas that "the Comforter, which is the Holy Ghost, whom the Father will send in my name, he shall teach you all things and bring all things to your remembrance, whatsoever I have said unto you." These, my friends, are the fundamental axioms of the Christian faith. The kingdom is based on love, not force, and God's revelation comes directly to his children. And if we have that love, it will be revealed in obedience.

Paul said, "Love never faileth." The one who is unmoved by love has closed the door to God. The one who opens the door to the love of God in Christ Jesus, responding to that love in faith, permits the abiding presence of the Holy Spirit to take up abode in his life. If he's in charge, the result will be obedience.

How many areas can you think of right now in which you have

been disobedient to God? A lot of them, if you're honest. Beloved, that's where to start. That's where revival begins. Revival starts when disobedient, hardhearted, cold, backslidden Christians open their hearts in obedience and say, "By the grace of God I'll turn from sin and turn to Jesus Christ!" That's when he comes in. That's when he reveals his will. That's when he makes you know what he wants you to do.

Some could start Sunday night in the evening worship service. You know, Sunday night is still Sunday. That's still God's day. Do you believe that? God's day isn't over at 12:00 noon, as you walk out of church. You've got as much responsibility to God on Sunday night as you have Sunday morning. There's as much of an opportunity for Christian growth and learning and service at night as there is in the morning. Sunday is God's holy day, and if you're only giving God a part of it, you might start right there. That's a good place to begin being obedient.

What about when God's people come together on prayer meeting night? No, there isn't anything in the New Testament that says you must come to church on Wednesday night for prayer meeting, but the New Testament does say, "Men ought always to pray, and not to faint!" And there are certain values of corporate prayer that can't be gained anywhere else. You can begin in the obvious ways if you really want to be obedient. If the love of God in Jesus is in your heart, that's what you'll do.

Remember Judas'—

Responsibility.

Judas Thaddaeus Lebbaeus, son of James, was in the process of learning what Jesus came into the world to do. Because it's the same process in which you and I are involved, we need to learn the same lessons he learned.

There is no lesson more important or more needed than the lesson of obedience. Our Lord placed the future of his kingdom on the foundation of obedient, loving response. He could have brought in his kingdom by calling forth legions of angels and wiping the Romans off the face of the earth. He could have called down fire from heaven upon his enemies and decimated them. That's what you and I would have done. If we had that power we would have used it, but that isn't the kind of kingdom Jesus came to establish. If he had established a kingdom based on force, you and I would not have been involved. Force could have been invoked by celestial power, and human beings wouldn't have figured in it. That would have left us with no need to pray, no need to attend the worship services, no need to sacrifice, no need to witness, no need to give our money, no need to die, but that's not Christ's way. Christ chose to work through obedient human beings, people who love him.

It wasn't up to Judas to determine the game plan of the kingdom of God. Jesus didn't say, "Now Judas, you figure out how this ought to be done, then let us know and we'll do it your way." All that Judas was responsible for was carrying out orders. That's all we are responsible for today.

We're of the same impatient stripe as Judas. Oh, we vaguely believe that God's going to be the ultimate victor, but we want God to win this fight right now! Why doesn't God stop that hostile bunch of enemies over in the Middle East, who for millenia have fussed, fought, killed each other? Why doesn't God do something? Why doesn't God step in over there in Northern Ireland where some people, in the name of the Christian religion, are acting like pagans? Why doesn't God stop all that? Well, that represents the effort we make to write God's game plan. We want God to do it our way. We have the attitude, "Why doesn't God do something?" Listen to me, I have news for you. That's not the question! The question is, why don't you and I do something? That's God's game plan. He's left it in our hands and promised us the power with which to accomplish the task. He's promised us his presence. He said, "I'll never leave you or forsake you." He said, "Lo, I am with you alway, even until the end of the world." We are responsible to Christ for the work of the kingdom and it's our sole duty to be faithful and obedient day in and day out.

That's the lesson that Judas, the son of James, learned. He learned that he was personally responsible. That's the same lesson we need to learn. No one of us can evade that responsibility, no one of us is exempt from it, but each one has an obligation to God to reveal his love through obedience.

XII
JUDAS ISCARIOT
John 12:1-8

Our study of certain of the twelve apostles has been hampered by a dearth of biographical material. That's not our problem in the study of Judas Iscariot. Our problem in this study is that we come to it with preconceived ideas. Most of us have already decided what we believe about Judas. The name itself is identified with the most infamous traitor in history.

Traitors always get a great deal of publicity. Shakespeare capitalized on this in a number of his plays, for his villains are as well known as his heroes. Shylock is as famous as Portia, Iago as Othello, Brutus as Julius Caesar, Lady Macbeth as Banquo. We often use the name Benedict Arnold as an adjective, for in American history he stands high on the list of traitors.

The most probable meaning of the name Iscariot is a place name. The Hebrew word *ish* means "man" and "Kerioth" was the name of a town. It's likely that Iscariot means "a man of Kerioth." If that be the case, Judas was the only non-Galilean among the twelve apostles. Kerioth was located in the far south of Judea, near the border of Idumea.

Could it be that Judas felt he was a misfit? Did he consider himself to be the proverbial square peg in the round hole? Persons who have that feeling often are guilty of bizarre actions. When an individual feels he's out of step with the rest of his contemporaries, he's likely to be guilty of variant behavior.

I invite you to consider his—

Position.

Questions come quickly to our minds in this study. Why would Jesus offer this man a position as one of the twelve select apostles? As if that question were not enough to occupy us, our minds also suddenly question why Judas would want to be one of the twelve. If he was not genuinely saved, if he really was not committed to Christ, why would he want to be one of his close followers?

On many occasions Jesus discouraged those who misinterpreted or underestimated the demands of the kingdom. He never failed to nail down the fact that kingdom citizenship required self-denial, the bearing of one's cross in self-abnegation. Judas was not unaware of that. Why did he even want to be one of the twelve? I'm sure you have considered some of these questions and possibly your mind has been satisfied with the same answer that satisfies me. I believe Judas originally followed Jesus out of a deep heart-hunger. I'm convinced Judas understood Jesus Christ had what he needed most. I hold that to be the reason Judas followed our Lord. He had no pressure upon him to be saved, no one pushing him to serve Christ. It was his own choice, and undoubtedly that choice was made on the basis of an understanding of personal need.

Clear your minds of preconceived ideas, and remember, please, that Judas never committed any crime for which an American judge or jury would convict him. He wasn't guilty of breaking any civil law ever placed on any books. He merely betrayed a friend. He sold out to that which he loved most. He would be considered by most of us a sharp businessman. He knew how to turn a fast buck. He knew where the action was and how to make money.

Judas was a religious man. He was the kind of man most churches would consider a wonderful prospect for church membership. He had the ability to make money. Outwardly, it was obvious that he was religious. He followed the right people. He was in the company of the most committed people of that day. Everyone knew who his associates were. But it's apparent as we read the Gospel accounts of this man that he was afflicted with a mania for money. That was the consuming passion of his life, the god to whom he bent his knee in obeisance. It's equally clear that he never yielded that mania to the transforming touch of Jesus Christ.

I have known men, men who had great money-making ability, who capitalized on that innate talent for the glory of God. I've known men who said, "I can't lead in public prayer. I can't teach a Sunday School class or a lesson. I can't stand before people and take positions of leadership, but God has given me the ability to make money, and I'll use that for God's glory," and they've given generously of their material assets for kingdom causes. Judas never reached that point. His love for money began and ended with himself.

Don't think Judas surprised Jesus when he betrayed him. Our Lord was not taken unaware. In John 6:70 Jesus asked, "Have not I chosen you twelve, and one of you is a devil?" Rather than getting into the argument of whether Judas was once saved and then lost, whether or not he fell from grace, just take the words of Jesus. Jesus said a long time before the betrayal that Judas was a devil. John, the author of the Gospel, adds these words, "He spake of Judas Iscariot the son of Simon: for he it was that should betray him."

Another question I had to clear out before coming to an understanding of Judas was whether or not Jesus called him in order for him to be a traitor. If he did, then Jesus encouraged Judas to sin. I don't believe our Lord did that. I believe Judas had free choice, that he had as much possibility of becoming what the other eleven became as any one of them. His downfall came as a result of a series of wrong choices. The god of his life demanded these choices, and when he made them, destruction and chaos were inevitable.

Remember the—

Problem

—as we seek to focus on it both in his life and in our own. In the choice between Judas and Jesus, Judas chose Judas. The text reveals that Judas "had the bag." This was a reference to what was probably a leather purse in which the money owned by the apostles was kept to meet common needs. Judas kept the bag, for he was the treasurer of the twelve. John adds that Judas was a thief (12:6). Out of the common treasury of the apostles Judas allowed some of the money, which partially was rightfully his own, to stick to his fingers.

I have appreciated a recent campaign by merchants to combat shoplifting. The tragedy is that most shoplifters are not destitute. They steal to fulfill some other need. Judas was not hungry. He was not deprived of anything necessary for his existence. He stole from some other motivation.

Some shoplifters think the world owes them a living, that that merchandise on those counters which they want they must have, whether or not they have the money to buy it. Sometimes they feel they have been abused by a store or a clerk, or maybe they've received shoddy merchandise. Sometimes they justify themselves this way.

I'm certain Judas must have been guilty of that same kind of rationalization. He'd undoubtedly gotten his own consent to steal out of the bag. Maybe he said, "After all, I've gone to some degree of trouble for these other fellows. I deserve this. This is rightfully mine. I'm the one who has gone to the effort to keep up with this, and they ought to be paying me something." Maybe that's the way he got his own consent to steal.

Surely he loved Jesus. At least, he had some appreciation for him, but when it came to a choice between Jesus and money, Judas chose what he loved most. He loved money most and that's where his choice lay. His love for money grew over the months that he followed Christ, and as that love for money grew it pushed Jesus out.

I'm saying to you that's the scarlet sin in the lives of citizens in my city and yours. I can name scores of families that were active in programs of churches and in their service for Christ until they began making money. The richer they got, the less spiritual they became. Their love for money and the things money can buy pushed Jesus out. They are not one whit different from Judas Iscariot! That's precisely what happened to him.

How many families can you name who served Christ faithfully until they got enough money to buy a place at the lake? Then suddenly absenteeism set in, an absence from the place of worship, an ignoring of the things of the Spirit; Christian growth ceased and spiritual atrophy set in. They withered and died in their testimony because love for money pushed Jesus out.

This is exactly what our Lord taught in the parable-of the rich fool (Luke 12:16-21). The King James Version says: "This night thy soul shall be required of thee." A more literal translation of the original is, "This night these things are requiring thy soul of thee." What things? Stocks and bonds, oil leases and oil wells, houses and lands, crops and barns—those things a man loves which are jealous when served as gods. Those gods won't allow a rival. They'll crowd out Jesus Christ. They'll crowd out the things of the Spirit.

Judas' greed for money required a decision. It was a decision between Jesus Christ and thirty pieces of silver! In modern money that would be equivalent to twenty bucks. Most of what shoplifters steal is worth less than that. Can you imagine making a decision to compromise one's integrity and lose one's soul for twenty miserable dollars! That's what he loved, and when the choice was made that's what he chose. Money was Judas' big problem, and it's the problem in the life of nearly every one of us.

We complain about some of the social evils. We name them one after another. Let me remind you that money is at the heart of the problem in every social evil. Gambling—a love for money at the heart of it. Prostitution—it's a love for money at the heart of it. The drug traffic—it's a love for money on the part of those who are pushing drugs. Whiskey—it's a love for money on the part of those who sell that commodity and blight the lives and destroy the homes of Americans with it. A love for money. The same thing goes for beer and wine, and all other alcoholic beverages.

Why would a person operate a lounge where mixed drinks are sold, where fights occur, and where people blight the talents that God has given them, and benumb their ability to think and act as human beings? Why would you sell something that will make a man act like an animal? Money! It's love for money that stands at the root of every social evil we know.

The problem is so great it creeps into your life and mine. The terrible, terrible danger is that you and I are also capable of doing exactly what Judas did. His sin didn't occur suddenly. It was not a spur-of-the-moment decision he made. His sin came as a result of a number of wrong choices. It developed over a period of time.

That sin grew in the life of Judas in spite of the warning given through every word Jesus spoke and every deed he did. Sixteen of the thirty-eight parables, almost 50 percent of them, have to do with the sin of the love of money and man's stewardship of material possessions. Judas heard everything Jesus said on the subject, but he hardened his heart and made his ultimate decision on the basis of a number of other decisions he had made. He'd already made his decision to steal out of the purse; so when it came to a decision to sell Jesus, he made the same kind of decision, the same tragic sin.

Undoubtedly Judas understood what Jesus had said, just as some of you have understood the gospel when it's been preached again and again. Judas lacked the moral courage to decide. He was so in love with money he had decided that whatever it took to get it was worth it. Any compromise he needed to make to get money would be worthwhile. So his decisions just followed one after another, all in the same direction, the direction of a love for material things.

Judas could not be trusted with money belonging to others, the eleven apostles. We sneer at that. We conclude if we were given that sort of trust we would be faithful to it. Yet many religious people who are church members in good standing can't be trusted with God's money. God pours it out upon us and like Judas, we steal what he said is his. The Bible doesn't mince words about it,

"Will a man rob God?" R-o-b. Will a man shoplift from God? The prophet Malachi flatly asserted they will! They are doing it every day when God's people steal God's tithe and fail to bring it into God's storehouse as he commanded.

So you see, Judas' problem is not unusual. It's a problem faced by just as many people today as in any other generation. Unless we check that cancerous sin of greed and love for material things, our end is going to be like that of Judas—destruction, chaos, and eternal hell. We make those little decisions day by day, paycheck after paycheck, every opportunity that we have to walk up and down the aisle of a store and perhaps steal something. We make those little decisions then, but they build up and get bigger and bigger. Finally we'll make the ultimate decision just as Judas did, and I can guarantee you it will not be out of character with the rest of life. It will be in the same direction, in keeping with the god to whom we have committed our lives.

Remember Judas'—

Potential.

This is one of the great tragedies in this whole situation. Judas could have been a man of God. Doesn't that break your heart? He had the possibility of doing as much good for posterity as he did evil. He's never been forgotten, but he's remembered in infamy. He could have been remembered in honor and in deference.

Jesus reminded us that where our treasure is our hearts are. This is as true today as ever. If our treasure is money and the things money can buy, that's where our hearts are. When the chips are down and decisions are made, that's the line along which we'll make our decisions.

Perhaps Jesus used Judas as a warning to you and me. Yes, there was a hypocrite among the twelve. People often say to me, "Preacher, there are hypocrites in your church." Sure there are. Jesus never told us otherwise, for even among the twelve apostles one was a hypocrite. Can't we thank God the other eleven didn't use Judas as an excuse? Can't we thank God they didn't say, "I'm not going to be seen where the hypocrite is! If he's going to follow Jesus, I'm not!" Thank God they didn't, even though they knew Judas. They understood him but remained faithful to Jesus in spite of him. Eleven out of the twelve were faithful to our Lord, and that's the fact that needs emphasizing. No greater warning could be given you and me than this.

Judas was a deeply religious man. He could be classified as a sympathizer, but the fact is many religious people are lost. It was a religious man who betrayed our Lord. It was religious leaders who brought about the crucifixion of our Lord. Don't think that being religious is adequate. It isn't.

Following the betrayal and the payoff, Judas came back to try to undo what he had done. He brought the money and he threw it at them, not wanting to keep it, knowing he had betrayed innocent blood. He was aware of the fact that Jesus Christ, the sinlessly perfect Son of God, was innocent. He admitted Jesus was a man of excellent character and blameless in the ways of men, but friend, that's not to be misconstrued as salvation. You can have the highest opinion of Jesus and be as lost as Judas was. Our Lord was not just innocent, our Lord is the Son of the living God and the Savior of all the world!

When he was called to be an apostle, Judas had the potential of becoming a strong, stalwart witness for our Lord like Simon Peter and Andrew, James and John, and all the others, but he wanted to hold on to the Savior and silver simultaneously.

Modern psychiatry describes this ancient malady as schizophrenia. "Schizo" means to divide or to split. "Phrenia" refers to a disease of the mind. Fence straddlers and doubleminded persons end up the way Judas did. New Testament Christians were characterized in the words of Paul when he said, "This one thing I do." Paul was no schizophrenic. Judas was. Judas wanted to hold onto money and the things money can provide while trying to hold onto Jesus at the same time. You can't do it. One will ultimately crowd out the other.

Before you severely condemn Judas or censure him, remember the words of Jesus when he suggested to a group of men one day that the one who was without sin should cast the first stone. Let's not turn thumbs down on Judas harshly, but let's apply the lessons of the Word of God to our lives and be honest enough to admit what we know to be true.

In the garden of Gethsemane, when the soldiers laid hands on our Lord, Jesus called Judas "friend." His forgiveness was offered, but it was rejected. Even at that late hour, after Jesus Christ had been taken prisoner, he still was willing to offer Judas pardon and peace. Judas rejected it and went out to take his own life and go out into eternity separated forever from the presence of God.

Today the offer of Jesus Christ is extended to you and me in love and pardon. We may have betrayed him, but he loves us. He doesn't love you any less because you have betrayed him. He doesn't love me any more than he does you because I'm a preacher. He loves every one of us the same. The most spectacular fact about the Christian faith is that "while we were yet sinners Christ died for us." He loves you though you've sinned, though you've turned to other gods to follow them, though you've made bad choices; he loves you and his arms are extended to you in love and forgiveness. All you must do is to accept what he offers.

Date

Code 4386-04, CLS-4, Broadman Supplies, Nashville, Tenn.,
Printed in U.S.A.

Date